Joyful Living

A Story of Faith and Family

By

Robyn Scott-Johnson

ISBN 978-0-578-90397-2
Library of Congress Control Number 2021908804
Cover Design by Germancreative
Formatting by Suzette Vaughn
Editor Deborah T. Salahu-Din, M.A.
Photograph by Necole Salley

Acknowledgments

To My Mother, Grandmother, Sister and all the Women who nurtured me along the way. I dedicate this Labor of Love to you all.

My village of strong prayer warriors who loved, supported and encouraged me every step of this journey, it was those prayers that gave me strength.

My beloved Husband Carvon and my beautiful daughters Janai and Jayla, this book is dedicated to the three of you. God chose me and I answered the call. My love for each of you is unconditional.

Contents

The Beginning of my Faith

What God has for you is for you.

A beautiful baby girl was born on June 28, 1963 to a young couple named Ada, affectionately called "Peaches," and James, affectionately called "Scotty." My mother was a very attractive woman with beautiful long black wavy hair. Her face a smooth caramel color, dark brown eyes and a drop-dead gorgeous shape at five feet, two inches tall. She was a deep thinker and always had something profound to say. My father was tall; six feet, two inches, light skinned and very lean. He was a smooth operator, always smiling, laughing and profiling for all to see.

The couple met in high school and spent most of their time going to the movies, dances and just hanging out in the neighborhood, like two teenagers in love. My parents loved to dance, and my father was really good at doing the Cha Cha and my Mother loved to Bop. Their love songs were Gee Wiz by Carla Thomas and Jimmy Mack by Martha Reeves and the Vandellas. The family legend told to me was, on October 1, 1962 at my Aunt Lorraine's twenty-first birthday party, I was conceived.

Once my mother became pregnant in her senior year of high school, I often thought about her decision at that time to keep me. She had her whole life ahead of her and she put it all on hold to keep me. "Would this be a dream deferred or part of God's Master Plan?"

The day that I was born my mother decided to paint the fence in the backyard of my grandparents' home on Allison Street in West Philadelphia. I guess she thought she had time because her due date was July 4. The fumes of the paint sent my mother into early labor, with very painful contractions. It was obvious I did not like the smell and was ready to make my grand entrance.

My grandmother was very calm as she got my mother ready to go to the hospital. My father was at work and was notified to meet us there, and according to my grandmother, a very handsome police officer escorted us with sirens blazing. I am going to stick with that scenario, because that's just the way I would want to be announced, "The love child is coming!"

My mother had just celebrated her eighteenth birthday in May, and my father was soon to be twenty in July. The two of them did not plan on becoming parents at such a young age, but God makes no mistakes.

My father made my mother laugh, and he made her feel good about the life the two of them would have together as a young couple. He was a great talker and had many dreams of going to college and having his own business. He really was not sure what kind of business, but it all sounded good to the high school girl who was so in love with the handsome young man.

My father saw my mother as a beautiful, strong woman and he needed someone who could resist his bullshit. He was used to getting his way from his nine older sisters and mother, whom I heard spoiled him rotten.

My maternal grandparents, George and Esther, were influential in rearing me. I stayed with them from birth while my mother attended junior college, and my father worked. Both were figuring out how to be new parents. Parenting is difficult at any age, but it can be done if there is love and a village supporting you and the child. I was told that my grandparents had lost a baby girl the year before I was born, and both of them, especially my grandmother, were heartbroken. She was excited and felt it was a blessing having a new baby in the house. I felt their love from the day I was born and my grandparents and I had a special bond that I will cherish forever.

My parents were married shortly after I was born and for two years; I was the love child that everyone wanted to hold, coddle, kiss and show off to their young friends. My father, especially, took me to visit all of his family members so they could see the cute little girl with sandy blonde hair and a big smile. I was born happy and smiling, the child that never cried and always gave hugs and blew kisses. I was talking and walking at an early age and kept everyone busy as they tried to keep up with me.

My mother was soon to have another baby and even though I was only two-years old, I was excited about becoming a big sister. I remember my brother Jimmy coming home from the hospital and how cute he looked all bundled up and cozy. It was November of 1965 and we had just celebrated Thanksgiving. He was a cute little baby boy with a head full of black curls. My mother was so happy to have a son. There was something special between the two of them, a very strong and loving bond.

As we got older, we did everything together and I have several pictures of us dressed like twins. But he was not like me at all, he cried all the time. They started calling him "The Town Crier." He was always following me around and would cry if he didn't see me, but I made sure he could always find me, I loved my baby brother.

My early childhood was filled with many family gatherings and the normal day to day activities. I loved school, dolls, playing dress up, dancing and going "Bye Bye" as I would call it. My bags were always packed and ready to visit with my aunts or travel with my beloved grandparents. My Pop Pop loved fishing and would take his yellow boat which he named Robin to Virginia, (his hometown), those vacations were some of my greatest memories.

My grandparents were my protectors as if they knew, I needed protection. My grandfather was my favorite and I would just light up around him. I always felt happy and special around him, he always gave me all of his attention. I could remember him coming home from work and I would run outside to greet him before he would get to the front door. He always had a smile for me and would pick me up and say "How is my special girl." I would just laugh and kiss him all over his face, he was always gentle, kind and loving to everyone, especially me.

My parents struggled as a young couple, and my father began drinking heavily. I think he began drinking after his mother, Virginia, passed away in 1962. She was the matriarch of the family, who reared eleven children and others from the neighborhood. My grandmother Virginia, who I was named after, was beautiful, smart, strong-willed and a great cook, who loved to entertain family and friends. Virginia would feed everyone and anyone that walked in her house, she was the real "Big Momma." I never got a chance to meet her, but I feel her spirit and my aunts always said I remind them of her.

My father was a lot like her, he was the life of the party and would escort all his sisters to all of their dances and was just fun to be around. He was the baby boy and all nine of his sisters loved and adored him. He was, afterall, their favorite.

I know my father's drinking put a strain on my mother and our family, but she was determined to make the young marriage work. She tried to change him but knew she could not, you can't fix what you did not break and he was broken.

I liked having a brother, but what I really wanted and prayed for was a baby sister. When my mother became pregnant again, I told her I would be her little helper. My sister Tina was born in early October, 1969, and I was the happiest six-year-old little girl in the world. I helped my Mom with everything from feeding, changing diapers, and even rocking her to sleep. She was a quiet baby with a calmness that you could see and feel. Tina wasn't a fussy baby like my brother, I fell in love with her at first sight. I secretly became her second mommy, and I was going to make sure she was well taken care of.

For a couple of years we were a "normal family" of five, living what I thought was my dream, a dream that began to slowly shatter, piece by piece. I always saw life differently according to my mother. I created what I wanted my life to look like early as a child, and began to believe and live it everyday. I just wanted everyone to be loved, happy and together. I remember our family trips to Coney Island visiting my great Aunt Gracie and how much fun we would all have. My father loved Aunt Gracie, I think she reminded him of his mother Virginia. She didn't have any children of her own and we became her family. Those were the only family vacations and memories we all spent together.

Life started to get the best of my mother, and she began having difficulties handling all of the demands of being a wife and a mother of three small children, with no help from my father. I can remember her crying all the time and me putting my little arms around her and telling her everything would be okay. I was young and still believed that everything would be okay even though it wasn't.

Once my parents separated, we all moved to West Philadelphia, into an apartment around the corner from my grandparents. I loved that neighborhood and all the kind people who lived around us. I knew my mother dreamed of having her own home, and all of us having our own bedrooms. Our very small apartment had only two. My brother and I shared a small room with bunk beds, and my sister slept with my mother. I tried to help as much as I could, making sure my brother and sister were dressed and fed in the mornings before we left to go to school.

My father would often come to visit and take us to see his family and friends. I never wanted to go and be my father's show and tell piece, so many times I would stay at home with my mother or go to my grandparents. We stayed in this home for a few years as my mother saved and worked hard to provide the best for us, still dreaming of her own home one day.

In the summer of 1972, we moved to "Frazier Lane" as I liked to call it. It was really Frazier Street and it had four-bedrooms. My mother's dream of each of us having our own bedroom was now a reality. I was very excited and proud of my mother for the many sacrifices she made for her dreams to come true. Our home was on a tree-lined block of row homes with neatly manicured front lawns and porches with decorated awnings. It was a beautiful home that had a fake fireplace in the living room and arches between the dining room and the kitchen. My favorite part of the home was the mirrored built in coat rack in the vestibule with a seat that opened for storage. We only had one bathroom at the time we moved in, but later my mother remodeled the entire house. She added another bathroom, tore down walls to create a more open floor plan, and gave herself a brand-new kitchen.

Life was starting to become normal again for the "four of us," but I knew my mother missed my father, her soulmate and the only man she loved. They would continue to see each other as if they were never separated, they were inseparable. I didn't understand this love that they had for each other.

My father and I really never bonded, I never had the same feelings for him that I had for my grandfather whom I loved, adored and admired. I never got excited when my father came to see us like my brother and sister did, so I always made excuses not to see him. I remember the nights they argued for hours and my mother crying all night. Those memories stay with a child forever. My mother asked us all one day what we thought about my father moving in with us. Everyone screamed with excitement and was happy with my mother's news, except me. I was very upset and could not believe what I was hearing, and just looked at her, and said nothing. I think this was a test from God, our Sunday school lesson that morning was on honoring our parents, a message I needed to hear.

My parents eventually renewed their vows and my father was now living with us again. I tried to be happy for my mother because she was so happy and in love. In the beginning I would ignore him as if he was not there. As I look back on it now, I was as rude as rude could be. I should have gotten my "butt beat" for how nasty my behavior was, but of course, I didn't. I eventually softened up because I saw how it affected my mother and siblings. I loved my mother and did not want her to be upset or unhappy anymore. He made many promises to my mother and many he never kept.

I was attending Junior High school in 1976 and was entering into the seventh-grade, the age where boys start looking at you with that mischievous look. I was very uncomfortable with the names they would call me. I was a skinny, flat chested girl with long hair and no shape at all. I saw all my friends developing in areas that I could only wish for. I really prayed for God to fix me, I didn't understand why I didn't have the same body as my girlfriends. However, I had a bubbly personality and always had friends around me. I was very active in student government and took dance lessons at The Philadelphia School of Dance Arts. Socializing was definitely my favorite and I spoke to everyone I would see and meet.

At home I made sure Jimmy and Tina did homework before my parents arrived home from work, and I started dinner for the family every night. My mother was not the best cook, but she tried her best. My father actually knew his way around the kitchen and his meals were very tasty, especially breakfast. Saturday morning breakfast was always scrambled eggs with cheese, sausages, and his famous home fried potatoes. I had several cookbooks from the library and would try different recipes for the family to enjoy. I loved to get all the ingredients together and start preparing the meals and the weekly food shopping my mother and I would do together every Thursday night. It was our special "mother daughter" time and I loved every moment with her. My mother always had wise words to share with me and I would listen and learn, knowing one day I would share with my own daughters.

Things seemed to be "normal" in our home until one morning when I wasn't feeling well and stayed home from school. I was sitting alone on the couch in the living room watching TV. My father came and sat next to me and asked "how I was feeling." He put his hand on my shoulder and began rubbing them. I thought nothing of that until I could feel his hand slowly sliding down my pajama top and touching my breast. I jumped up and looked at him and he said "it was an accident." It wasn't an accident! I looked right at this man who was still sitting and commanded, "Don't you ever touch me again!" I was angry and he knew it. I said, "You are a sick man. I am your daughter, what is wrong with you?" I ran to my bedroom and locked the door. I cried, I screamed and cried some more, never once did he come and apologize or see how I was doing.

My father, who should have been my protector, was now the predator. I stayed in my room crying until everyone came home later that evening. My mother came into my room and asked how I was feeling, and I surprisingly said, "I am feeling better." I knew I was lying to myself and to my mother, I was not ready to tell her yet, so I waited and said nothing.

Things became very tense in our home. My father and I didn't speak a word to one another. He would stare at me as if he were undressing me with his eyes, and that made me very uncomfortable in my own home. Every part of my body tightened up when he was around me. I avoided him as much as I could and wondered if my mother saw this behavior. She had to notice my disdain for this man, it was very obvious.

I didn't like to bathe, take showers or even go to the bathroom if he was in the house. I felt like he would find a way to watch me through a crack in the wood of the bathroom door or the small keyhole. Even though I would lock the door, I could hear him get out of his bed, and the sound of his bare feet would let me know he had stopped at the bathroom door and was watching me. I could only imagine his six foot, two inch frame, crouching down looking through any crack he could find to get a glance at my young innocent body. I quietly took a brown towel from the linen closet and hung it over the back of the door to cover up the cracks and the small keyhole so he could never see any parts of my body ever again. I would always scream "I know you are there!" and "You disgust me!"

Many nights I cried out to God, "How can a father do this to his own child?" I would be in bed crying into my pillow so no one could hear me. It was at that moment I could feel something come over me that was so powerful, comforting and peaceful. I believed it was God telling me that your Heavenly Father will always love and protect you. I felt God's presence, and it was very comforting to me.

My idea of a good father was to be God-fearing, protective, strong, loving, caring and respectful. He would teach, provide and would be a role model for his family. My mother was that strong figure in our household. My father loved the streets and gambling much more than he loved the family that he was abandoning. He began drinking heavily once again, which infuriated my mother. She would ask him to do many things around the house, and of course, he wouldn't do any of them. One morning before he left for work, she asked him to set a mousetrap, he ignored her request. My mother, who was very mischievous, caught the mouse herself and put it in a covered plate on the stove. Guess what she served him for dinner that night? We all heard his loud screams that night. She would do some crazy things just to get back at him for coming home late and drunk. She would rearrange the bedroom furniture so he could fall, as he was trying to get into the bed. I would be in my room laughing, and the next morning nobody said a word.

This behavior went on until my mother could not put up with it anymore. She had three children she had to think about and one of them was more than happy to say, "let him go." I wanted to tell my mother how I was feeling and the secret that I had kept. I wanted to tell her the truth, and I knew I would have to tell her sooner than later. They began to argue more and more, and one night I had to break up one of their arguments. I had to physically come between the two of them and console my mother once again.

After my father left the house that evening, I got my mother to her bedroom, and it was at that moment, I looked squarely at her, and told her what my father had done to me. It was the hardest thing for me to do, because I knew how much she loved this man. I began crying, not for me, but for her. I looked at her face, and saw sadness, helplessness and a broken heart, something I never wanted to see again. My mother didn't question me, it was as if she knew my secret and now the truth was finally out. She took me in her arms and that night we both just cried. We never spoke about that night ever again.

The next morning, she told my father to pack up his clothes and leave her house. This was the wake up call he needed and he immediately committed himself into an intensive treatment program for alcoholics. Once he completed the program, he never took another drink, and he began counseling others who suffered with alcohol and other addictions.

My mother, now single again, continued to support our family. She believed her children deserved the best education and transferred us to Robert E. Lamberton, a Magnet School outside of our school district. That was not the only thing that changed that summer of 1977. I asked my mother if I could legally change the spelling of my name from Robin to Robyn. I knew this was more than just a letter change in my name. Exercising the right to choose the spelling of my name sparked my recognition of my power as a young woman. She agreed but never wrote my name with a "y".

I was happy to be attending Lamberton High School and on the very first day, I walked into my ninth-grade homeroom and looked for anyone who looked kind. I saw one girl sitting with her hands folded and kindness written all over her face. I walked towards her and introduced myself as Robyn with a "y" and then asked her if she would be my new best friend. Call it a God thing, but I now know it was God who introduced me to Damita Richardson, my lifelong friend and sister.

I also knew attending Lamberton would be the change my brother needed, he was very bored in his current sixth-grade class and needed to be disciplined and challenged more academically. This boredom got him in trouble all the time as he acted out in class and tried to act tough in our neighborhood. My brother attended Lamberton for a couple of years and was doing very well academically and in sports. He was so smart that they tested and labeled him gifted, and he began taking advanced math and science courses in seventh-grade. My brother unfortunately started getting into trouble and was suspended several times, even though academically he had a bright future ahead of him. This school was strictly academics and would not tolerate his bad behavior and told my mother she would have to find an alternative school for him. My mother was running out of options for her troubled son. I had suggested that they send him to school and to live with my grandparents, who had now retired to Exmore, Virginia.

My grandfather was the hope we were looking for, and he proudly stepped up and said yes, bring him here. I prayed that my baby brother could be saved. Jimmy was not happy about the idea of going to school in Virginia, however, he excelled in his new high school. He had everything working in his favor and many well known colleges were interested in him because he excelled in math and science. West Point, MIT, University of Virginia, Drexel, Morehouse and the University of Pennsylvania were just to name a few. All he had to do was stay in school and stay in Virginia.

My grandfather had rules for his house and was a disciplinarian, just what my brother needed, some structure in his life. However, he was a "momma's boy" and cried to her that he wanted to come home and that our grandfather was too hard on him. My brother pulled on my mother's heartstrings, and he was on the next Greyhound bus home. This return marked the beginning of the end of my brother's life.

I was headed off to college to begin my life, and I left behind my brother, whom I loved and protected for most of our childhood. My brother came home angry and entered a life full of darkness and despair. He went back to high school but did not finish, and before long he was in and out of jail. My mother's heart was slowly breaking once again. Nothing seemed to go right for him, and no one could help him. I would see him when I would come home for school breaks and try to talk with him. My brother would always say that his life changed when I went away to college. I was his sister and his best friend, but this time I could not save my baby brother.

Four years at Clarion University went by very quickly, and I was graduating in May of 1985. It was a great celebration for my family, I would be the first to graduate college and that was something to celebrate. My family would be coming to see me walk across that stadium and accept my Bachelor of Science degree in Speech Communications.

I was expecting three car loads filled with my mother, Tina, Jimmy, Aunt Gracie, Aunt Sandra, Cousin Jenny, Cousin Jimmy, and their two children, Johanna and Jay J. My grandmother became ill, so she and my grandfather stayed back home. I was so excited and kept going to the window to see if I saw the cars driving up. I know I made my roommate Angel crazy, but she had been with me all four years, so she was immune to my craziness.

When I finally saw the cars driving up, I ran outside to welcome them. There was one car that I recognized right away, it was a shiny brown metallic Grand Prix. As I watched all the cars come around the circle, I saw my mother's face from the passenger side. She and I looked at each other, she could tell I was not happy about who was driving the car. How could she invite this man to my graduation and not tell me? His presence was not a surprise I wanted or deserved on this day. I became angry with her and realized my silence had been protecting her from the reality of an unspoken pain. Even though we had never spoken about that night, I still felt the way I did about my father and now I knew she had forgiven him.

All kinds of thoughts were going through my head, and I felt sick to my stomach. How could she do this to me on that day? I was so excited for graduation day to come and celebrate with my family, but now I had to face the one man I despised the most. As the cars were all parked and everyone began to exit with their excitement, I got myself together to greet them, giving big hugs and kisses to everyone. I even spoke to my father, because I did not want to make a scene, it was a day to celebrate and I was going to do just that.

It was a beautiful sunny day, and I will never forget how I felt walking down that ramp, wearing my black cap and gown and knowing that this day was finally here. I was so excited to hear all the names of my college friends who had become family to me. When my name was called, I could hear my family screaming with excitement. I knew my mother worked hard to make this day possible, so I looked over at her and said, "This is for you."

That beautiful day in May, we were also celebrating my mother's 40th birthday and Mother's Day. Our celebration continued that afternoon hosted by my dear friends Terri and Lloyd. They both worked at the college, and they became my surrogate family all four years I was there. My mother told me the day she dropped me off that she would not be back until I graduated from Clarion and she meant that.

I remember introducing my family to everyone and the look on Terri's face when I said my father's name. Terri was the only person in that room besides my mother that knew my secret. I confided in her one evening while we were at her home. It was just the two of us, and I remember saying to her I have something to share with you that I have not shared with anyone. She was so kind and gentle with me as I shared my story crying in her living room. We talked all night, and it felt so good to get it out in the open, finally. She assured me that I did nothing wrong and after talking to her that night, I realized I was beginning to heal and to forgive.

Everyone was having a great time at the graduation party getting to know one another, looking at pictures and enjoying the delicious food. I walked over to my parents and asked them to come outside with me. The look on both of their faces quickly turned to concern. Once outside I said to my mother, "I did not invite him here, and this is not the day that I would want to see his face. This is a man you have feelings for and love, not me." I then turned towards my father, I looked him in the face and said very calmly, "I didn't want you here. This is a part of my life that you know nothing about because you don't know me. I prayed for you and the only way I can move forward is to forgive you both." That day in May of 1985, I chose to forgive and I also discovered the power I had in me.

I moved back home that Spring to live with my mother, sister and brother as I began my new journey. After college I began working for TWA airlines with my best friend Angel. We traveled to countries like England, Spain, France and the Bahamas regularly living our best lives as single women.

I began dating Carvon in 1987, a handsome graduate student attending Drexel University. He captured my attention and heart with his big personality, his smile and a voice that once you heard it, you would never forget it. Carvon had just lost his father to cancer when I met him and I knew that he was in pain. I believed that God brought us together at the right time and I was trusting God's plan for the both of us.

It was nice having him around while Tina was a senior in high school and looking at colleges. He was a great help to my sister as she was going through the college process. He became the big brother to both my siblings, and I was hoping and praying he and Jimmy would form a brotherly bond. My siblings had always looked to me as their role model, even though they knew I was not perfect. They both knew I loved them and always had their best interest at heart. Tina graduated from high school and was off to attend the

University of Pittsburgh. My mother was so proud of her daughters.

It was October of 1988, a day that changed our lives forever. My mother, Tina and I always had a routine on Saturdays, we would clean the house and then the three of us would go shopping and have lunch. Since my sister was away at college, Carvon would now pick us up and tag along. Carvon came to the door that morning and my mother and I walked out together, but I ran back in the house to go to the bathroom. I heard the phone ringing, but I was hesitant to answer. Carvon was blowing the horn, but something told me to pick up the phone.

On the line was my Aunt Lorraine screaming, and I could not make out what she was trying to say. I asked her to calm down, and that's when I heard the most unthinkable words, "Your father has been killed!" She was hysterical on the phone crying and saying, "He is gone" over and over again. I froze right there in our living room holding the phone to my ear as the tears started falling down my face, and I could not move. I finally snapped out of it as my aunt kept calling my name "Robyn," "Robyn." I finally responded "I am here" and then she asked for my mother. I started crying all over again with the thought of telling her that my father was dead.

My mother had to identify his body, so my aunt gave me all the information that I needed and when I looked up, Carvon walked into the house. He could see that I was visibly shaken and upset. I got myself together and told him that my father had been found "murdered." It didn't even sound right to say, and I couldn't believe that I was saying it. I told him what we had to do and where we had to go. At that moment, so much was happening, I felt like it was a nightmare and I wanted to wake up. Then my mother walked into the house, and I looked at her face, she knew.

My cousin was waiting outside for us to go to the morgue so we could identify my father's body. I grabbed my mother, and we got into the back seat of the car as she began to cry. Once at the morgue, we identified my father, and my mother fell to the ground sobbing. My father was brutally murdered, "a victim of a robbery" we were later told by the detectives. His body was found near Cobbs Creek Park. Who could have done this and why? We got back into the car and drove home in silence.

As we pulled up to our house, the porch was filled with family and friends, the word was out. I brought my mother in the house to help settle her down, but so many people were constantly opening and closing the door and the phone would not stop ringing. This was truly a horrible nightmare. I tried calling my brother several times at work. I did not want him to hear this news from anyone, but me. I then called his friends to go get my brother and bring him home.

Things were happening so fast and I was thinking of everyone, especially my sister, who was away at college. I called Angel and the two of us flew to Pittsburgh the next day. When my sister saw me, she was happy at first and then she quickly looked frightened and asked "Why are you here, did something happen to mommy?" I told her, "No, it's daddy." She began to cry and asked, "What happened?" I just told her to get some clothes together, I am taking you home. Her roommate Alexis and her friends Selena, Dani and Angie were there supporting her.

We came home and began planning the funeral of our father. There was a lot of drama that week, but we got through it. My mother's heart was truly broken that day. She had lost the love of her life and would never find another. Our family was truly devastated by the loss of our father, which was compounded by the death of his sister the very next day, from a heart attack. The family had to bury a brother and a sister within a week of each other. We later learned the man responsible for my father's murder was convicted and is serving life in prison. It took some time for the healing to begin for our family as we finally had closure.

A few years passed and our families were getting ready to celebrate my marriage to Carvon in 1991. My beloved grandfather walked me down the aisle, and it was such an honor having him by my side. I had invited all of my father's siblings, and this was the first time we all were together since his death. I knew our wedding would bring them all joy. We were so happy that all of our loved ones were there to witness that special occasion. My sister had also graduated from college that same year. Our mother was so proud of her girls, we were both moving on and unfortunately, my brother was stuck, and only God could save him.

The Births of My Daughters

There is a special bond between a mother and daughter, one that will last a lifetime.

A mother's love starts at conception. I remember how excited I was when we found out we were having our first child. Carvon and I had been married for four years, and we were living our best lives as professionals in our careers, traveling and living carefree.

We had been trying for a year to conceive, and it was becoming very stressful. I kept thinking something was wrong with me. I cried out to God and kept asking "why?" Many of our friends who were married the same year, all were expecting, except me. I was tired of people asking, "When are you going to start a family? You know you are not getting any younger." It wasn't because of a lack of trying, because we were all the time.

Earlier in that year, my doctor discovered I had a large fibroid, and it needed to be removed from my ovaries. The doctor later told me that I would not have been able to carry a child with that benign tumor. I had the surgery and the next year we were having our first child. During my prenatal screening, a positive multiple marker for Down syndrome was detected. We then began the genetic testing and an amniocentesis was performed, a medical procedure used primarily in prenatal diagnosis of chromosomal abnormalities, fetal infections as well as determining one's gender. A small amount of amniotic fluid, which contains fetal tissue, is sampled from the amniotic sac surrounding a developing fetus. I informed the doctors that no matter the outcome, this child was a gift from God.

While we were visiting my grandparents over the Christmas holiday in 1994, we were notified by phone that despite the initial test, all the results were normal. We were also told that we were having a baby girl, our Christmas miracle. I began thanking God for this gift of life and preparing for our baby girl, whom I named Janai which means "God has answered" in Hebrew and who was due in May of 1995. I think I made everyone around me a little bit crazy, especially my family. I was the happiest woman in the world, my world that is.

Janai B was going to make her entrance on her terms, and she did just that on Wednesday May 24, 1995. She was already two weeks late, and I remember speaking with my doctor, making plans to come to the hospital to be induced. Carvon and I went out to dinner that Tuesday night for the last time as a family of two. My heart was so happy because we were going to come home from the hospital a family of three.

As we left our home that night I looked around Janai's room filled with love and with everything a princess could ever want. My baby shower was such a beautiful surprise, and yes, we received all things pink. We arrived at the hospital that Tuesday evening and met all the staff, and I chatted up with them all. We settled in the room and waited all night.

That morning I was induced, and again we waited. By this time my mother, sister and God mother had arrived, and I was happy to see them. Dr. Fang came to check on me several times that day. My water had not broken, so she did an internal exam, and I could see on her face, something was wrong. She looked at me and asked if I felt anything and I told her no. She informed us that Janai had turned and become breech, which meant an emergency C-section. I could see the fear on Carvon's face, and I just began to pray.

During the procedure, the umbilical cord was wrapped around her neck twice. Our baby girl was a fighter and came out fighting for her life. Janai weighed 8 pounds 15.8 ounces and was 20.5 inches long. Having had a C-section, I stayed in the hospital two extra days. Thank God I did, because the next day a cardiologist came in and rushed Janai to CHOP (Children's Hospital of Philadelphia). The doctor later told me they found a small hole in Janai's heart. Once they identified the condition and shared with us what needed to be done for her care, I began to pray for complete healing of our baby girl.

The next couple of months we were back and forth at CHOP seeing a cardiologist, and Janai was always being tested with monitors attached to her little body. We were told that the hole should close on its own while Janai was still an infant. If not, then surgery would be our next option. They would continue to monitor her for any heart related issues.

Once again in December, we were at CHOP for our monthly appointment and the staff would joke and say, "Here comes the princess with her entourage!" We went through the medical questions, physical examination, and the EKG as we had done several times. Our doctor looked at Janai and smiled and then told us the good news, the hole had closed. This was another Christmas miracle. What an entrance Janai B had made into the world. Our little princess with her beautiful dark brown eyes, curly hair, caramel skin, and chubby cheeks, who always smiled when you looked at her. The staff fell in love with this little girl named Janai.

I was obsessed with Janai and knew for her sake and my own we had to have another child. Janai was asking for a baby sister, and I told her if she starts sleeping in her own big girl bed, Mommy and Daddy would pray for a baby. Janai began to sleep all night in her own room, and sometimes I would hear her praying for a sister. Carvon wanted a son, and I just wanted a healthy baby. I must not lie, I wanted another princess. I did not let on to Carvon that I was praying for another girl. I woke up one morning, and I knew I was pregnant. I called my doctor to make the appointment and it was confirmed, we were having our second child in early August of 2000.

Because I was thirty-seven, and had complications from my first pregnancy, I was considered high-risk and another amniocentesis was scheduled. I remembered how I felt the first time going through this, and now I was looking at that little girl Janai, as we awaited my results for our second child. The office called informing me the good news, that all test were negative, and then asked, "Do you want to know the gender?" Janai was sitting next to me, so I put the phone between us so she could hear. Her little eyes became so wide, and she gave me the biggest smile, we were having princess number two. We were all very excited and I thanked God for blessing me with another healthy baby girl.

The pregnancy went well, and Janai was looking forward to the arrival of her baby sister, whom I named Jayla, which means "Special One" in Hebrew. We tried to prepare Janai as best as we knew how. She had been our one and only for five years. All our attention had been on her, and all our love was directed to her, and only her. My questions began, "God, how can I love another?" I remember lying next to Janai crying as she slept, promising her that I would always love her. She would never feel neglected and that she was very special, because God made her the oldest, just like me. I went on and on that night speaking to a sleeping child. I poured out my heart to her, and in some way, healing my own. I knew that I was going to have two daughters that would share my love, and that God had given me all that I would need, to love them both.

Jayla B was born August 7, 2000 by C-section and was healthy, happy and beautiful with a head full of hair. God never fails. As they put her in my arms, I could feel my heart beat with hers and I felt the same unconditional motherly love. I looked into my beautiful Jayla's dark brown eyes, and I saw them twinkle. God does give us enough love. Jayla seemed very happy and pleasant all the time. She slept through the night and did not fuss at all in the beginning. It wasn't until the age of three-months that she started having problems when I would feed her. This led me to ask questions during our visits with our pediatrician.

Her breathing seemed off, and I was concerned. We began by making changes to her regular formula, but that still did not satisfy her. Jayla was then diagnosed with Respiratory Syncytial Virus or (RSV) a virus that causes respiratory tract infections. This went on for a couple of months, and she always had a cold. After doing some research on my own, I began to see signs of asthma. No one wanted to diagnose her at this young age. I did what any good mother would do, I found a specialist who would listen to me.

Jayla was finally diagnosed with asthma and the treatments for this age were through a nebulizer. There were times when we had to give her treatments around the clock to keep her from being hospitalized. Everyone became an expert at giving Jayla her daily treatments. I have pictures of her as she got older sitting in her rocking chair, breathing through her mask, and swinging her little feet. I prayed that my baby girl would outgrow asthma one day. She suffered many nights, but through it all she remained happy and always had a smile on her face. She brought so much joy to the entire family, especially to Janai, her protective big sister. After several years with asthma, Jayla slowly had fewer and fewer attacks and eventually showed no more signs of having any respiratory problems.

Carvon and I were so proud of the girls' progress in school and in all their activities. I was a busy Mommy, working and keeping track of their daily activities. We were also happy that both girls loved the Lord, and looked forward to attending service on Sunday mornings. Our church was a big part of our lives, and life was good for "Team Johnson."

The Faith Walk Begins

God will prepare, provide and give you
peace that surpasses all understanding.

I had been working in the pharmaceutical industry with Bayer; as a senior sales representative, and loved every minute of what I did for fourteen years. My days were always busy with daily scheduled appointments, educating and promoting our product line of prescribed drugs to my preferred list of doctors, pharmacists, hospitals and drug stores.

Many of our products would be life changing for some and much needed for others. I made sure that I brought more value to my clients than most. I would go out of my way and talk to the patients about their healthcare needs and provide educational material. I wanted each of them to understand their own health conditions and how they could advocate for themselves. That was my greatest joy to be able to see many patients take charge of their health care needs and feel confident in doing so.

The Northeast Philadelphia and the surrounding suburban territories allowed me to develop long lasting relationships with the medical community that I served. I learned a lot about the industry from all with whom I came in contact and was very successful during my tenure.

In 2004, Bayer went through an industry merger, and I remember when I got the call and was told that I no longer had a position with the company. I hung up the phone and felt at peace. I began to think the Lord was preparing me for something greater. God knew what my life would look like and my steps were being ordered. I just didn't know all of his plans for me. My assignments began quickly and I was prepared.

Our family would soon experience many more family losses, beginning with my great Aunt "Gracie" in 2000 and my beloved "PopPop" in 2002. After the loss of my grandfather, my grandmother "GiGi" came to live with my mother. The two of them lived together for a couple of years on Frazier Lane until my grandmother's health started failing and it became difficult walking up and down steps. They eventually had to move into a two-bedroom condo with everything on one floor. The girls loved spending time after church with my mom "Peachy Peach" and my grandmother "GiGi." Those were the names the girls affectionately called them. My grandmother's health continued to fail, and we had to move her to a nearby nursing home facility. I became her caregiver and spent every moment with her until she passed away in August 2005.

That year my sister and I did all that we could do to comfort our mother as she grieved. I was grieving as well, and I knew that my number one fan was gone. It really was a tough year for all of us, but we got through with the love and support of family and friends.

That next year I had to have surgery, a hysterectomy. I asked my mother to come and stay with the girls while I was in the hospital. We went to pick her up, and I noticed that she didn't look good and she had this cough. My mother said she was okay and felt fine, just a little tired. We stopped and had lunch, but my mother didn't eat much that afternoon. The girls were so happy that "Peachy Peach" was coming to stay with them. They loved my mother and very much missed my grandmother "GiGi." The night before my surgery, I had a dream about death. When I woke up the next morning, I wrote letters to Carvon, Janai, Jayla and my mother. I placed each envelope in their bedrooms where they could all see them. I gave them all a hug and kiss as Carvon and I left for the hospital that day. I never spoke about the dream or the cards I left behind.

My surgery went well and I woke up in recovery realizing the dream was not about me. I stayed in the hospital for two days and spoke to my mother and the girls every day. When I came home, I had been given instructions not to drive or go up and down stairs and to just take it easy for a few weeks. That was going to be very hard for me to do. I still noticed that my mother's cough was getting worse and I was now concerned it was pneumonia.

My sister and I took our mother to the hospital, where they admitted her immediately and ran several tests. The results showed a large amount of fluid on her lungs, but after the fluid was drained, she was feeling better. I stayed all day with her as they ran test after test, and I questioned everything they were doing. I had my pen and pad recording all of her tests and results.

My mother had been in the hospital for several days as they continued to run a series of tests. It was a Thursday evening and I happened to be home and not at the hospital when my phone rang. It was my mother's primary care physician Dr. Murray, who proceeded to tell me that my mother had stage 4 renal cancer that had metastasized to her lungs and bones. He cried as he told me that she had only a few weeks to live. I was in shock as I listened to what he was saying to me, and held back my tears. I found the strength to thank him for being my mother's primary doctor, of whom she was very fond. I politely asked him to tell her she has cancer but nothing else and he agreed and did exactly what I asked.

We brought my mother home with us, and I got her right into Fox Chase Cancer Center for a second opinion. The next couple of days were busy with more tests, chemo, and radiation treatments, and eventually she was admitted back into the hospital. This went on for a total of three weeks. I would get up every morning, get the girls ready for school, and then go to the hospital and sit with my mother the rest of the day. When my sister would come in the evenings, the two of us would just rub her hands and pray, as we both sat beside her bed, listening to the soothing music coming from the TV.

The last words I said to my mother were "I love you and I did my very best" and she answered very softly "I know you did and I love you." My mother's last request to me was, "Please take care of my baby girl." I knew what she meant and I took those words to heart. My beloved mother passed away peacefully that evening of September 27, 2006 at age sixty-one. My dream that I thought was about me was about my mother. I thanked God again for letting me spend every day with her and for her not suffering long.

After my mother passed, I knew I needed a change. I wanted to get away from everyone. I felt such a loss and I could not explain my feelings. For the first time in my life, I felt alone and abandoned. I knew that I was sad and grieving and had to go through this painful process.

I forced myself to get up every day, get dressed and be a mother, the best mother I knew how to be. My mother and grandmother were my role models and I drew my strength from them. I prayed for direction and heard God tell me to stay home and nurture, love, protect and advocate for my daughters. Carvon would often ask me, "Are you ever going back to work?" and I would always laugh because I knew that being a mother was my job, the best job given to me by God.

In April 2009 at the age of eight, Jayla had accepted Christ in her life, and we all were so excited for her. Janai had accepted Christ in 2004. The whole family believed in God and knew that God was always with us and in control. Carvon and I always believed in rearing our children in the church, and we were blessed to belong to Christian Stronghold with Pastor Richardson and our entire church family who always supported, loved and prayed for us through our journey.

A Mother's Love for Jayla

In the blink of an eye,
I found my strength and voice.

It was a Friday evening May 1, 2009, right before the girls dance competition on Saturday, and Jayla was in her bathroom putting her hair up with a hair clip. The clip broke and something hit her in her right eye. I was not at home when this happened, I was out with a good friend Donna at our annual Philadanco performance. When I came home, Carvon and Janai informed me of the accident. I went into Jayla's bedroom and she was sleeping. I looked to see if there was any swelling or redness around her eye, and there was none.

Saturday morning when she awoke, I looked and saw that her eye was red, but she did not complain or tell us she was in any pain. I took the girls to their competition that day and Jayla, who had a cute little solo, did very well. Their group won high gold for their performance. Jayla was excited, but something was not right with her and she just did not seem herself.

We had to go back on Sunday because Janai's group was performing, and Jayla wanted to watch and support her big sister. Jayla was very quiet and sat on my lap the entire time with her head on my shoulders. I knew something was not right and after Janai's last dance, I drove to our community hospital's ER. Jayla was seen by the attending physician, who did a routine scan over her right eye and diagnosed her with a corneal abrasion (scratch on the eye). I was told that most abrasions heal rapidly without complications. She gave us a prescription for an antibiotic eye drop and told us to follow up with our ophthalmologist the next day. I brought Jayla home that evening and the next morning called our eye doctor, and she told me to bring her in, immediately. She agreed with me that something was wrong and it could be a scratched cornea, but did not have the proper equipment to examine her thoroughly. Dr. Lillian then instructed us to continue with the eye drops and see her in the office the next day.

That next morning she called after speaking with her colleague Dr. Paul, who agreed to examine Jayla right away. After his exam, he urged me to take her directly to Wills Eye emergency room in Philadelphia. I did not panic because Jayla was watching me very closely. Once we arrived, she was admitted quickly and given a CT Scan of her right eye. Carvon and I soon learned that her retina was detached and blood was accumulating in the back of her right eye and she would need surgery immediately. Everything was happening so quickly, and I needed a moment to process it all. I had not eaten that day, and my mind was racing. I was thinking of all sorts of scenarios and most importantly, I was scared for our baby girl.

We were transported that evening by ambulance to Jefferson Hospital. Once in our private room, I got Jayla as comfortable as possible and we began to pray. I held her all night until she fell asleep. I stayed awake praying and crying while I held my sleeping daughter. It had been 4 days since the accident. When morning finally came on Wednesday May 6, 2009, a young orderly and nurse took Jayla and I down to the operating room at

Jefferson Hospital. I saw on Jayla's face that she was very frightened. Carvon was there to meet us, and together we surrounded our daughter as they began to prep her for her first ever surgery. The anesthesiologist met with us and was so impressed with our Jayla. She was only eight years old but carried herself much older. He asked her if she had any questions and the only one she asked was "how were they going to put her to sleep and if she was going to feel anything." He was very gentle with her and assured her that she would be fine and that she was one of the bravest little girls he had ever met.

The surgeon Dr. Park, a Wills Eye Retina Specialist then arrived and spoke to Jayla about the surgery in terms that he hoped she would understand. He then put a red x on her right eye to mark it as the one he was to repair. They gave her some giggle juice to calm her down and then the mask went over her face. She cried and I assured her that she was going to be fine. I told Jayla to go to her happy place and stay there, and that God was with her. I held back my tears until she was inside the operating room and then and only then did I begin to cry in Carvon's arms.

He began to call our village of family and friends and inform them that she was in surgery and for everyone to please pray. The waiting seemed forever, as I looked around and saw many other families waiting for their loved ones to come out of surgery. Our baby girl was one of the youngest patients there that day and some were wondering what happened to her. I wasn't in the mood to talk about it, so I kept quiet and to myself.

I found a chair and made that my prayer chair, I sat drinking a cup of hot tea until Dr. Park came out of surgery and walked over to us. He looked at us and then asked if we would walk with him to a private room. I was very anxious to hear about the surgery, but the look on his face was hard to read. Once in the room he began to say the surgery went well, and he had repaired the detached retina. Dr. Park then paused and said; however, Jayla's lens was completely destroyed. He did retrieve the particle that did all this damage to her eye, but did not know if he was able to save her vision. "Oh my God!" I thought, my baby could lose her eyesight! This could not be, we were told she had a scratched cornea, and it would heal on its own.

Jayla was in the recovery room and was very groggy from the anesthesia, as I looked at our baby with this huge white bandage on her eye, my heart was aching for her. I quickly went to hug and kiss her and told her how proud I was of her for being so brave and strong. They kept her overnight to check for infections and to show me how to change the bandages. To me that was the easy part, giving her the four different eye drops at all different times was the challenge. When we finally came home, I knew that things were going to change for us all.

My first order of business was to get her eye drops on a schedule. I made a spreadsheet with each eye drop, the name, the color of the eye drop top, the doses, and the time she was to get them. I also had a column for one's initials. I was serious about my daughters' eye care schedule and home care. I also began writing everything down in a notebook as I had done when caring for my mother and grandmother. Jayla's eye drops were given around the clock. This too was not new for Carvon and me. Jayla had nebulizing treatments around the clock to keep her from being admitted to the hospital because of her asthma. This was our daily regimen for the first two weeks after Jayla's surgery.

We had to go back for our first follow up with Dr. Park on Tuesday, May 12. He told us that everything was healing, and it was too early to determine if any vision had returned. During that visit, I had shown him the spreadsheet for Jayla. He knew we were committed parents, and we would do whatever necessary for the care of our daughter. She had to keep a bandage on her eye for several weeks after surgery and that bothered her, as well as missing her friends and school.

I knew I had to get some normalcy back into her life. We had some of her classmates come and visit with her, and she was able to articulate her experience. They were in awe of her positive attitude. Our first outing was our annual Memorial Day BBQ at the Keltons's home. This was the first time many of our friends and family had seen Jayla since the accident. She had her patch on her eye and she was still full of life. I was happy to get out and socialize among our family and friends too. This was a good day for all of us, and we were feeling positive and hopeful.

Things quickly changed when we had our scheduled two-week Tuesday appointment. On May 26, we were told that the retina had detached again, and there was a lot of scar tissue that had to be removed. Dr. Park had informed us that this could happen because of the nature of the surgery. Jayla was scheduled for her second-surgery on May 27, to remove scar tissue and to put an oil bubble in her eye to keep the retina attached. The oil is a clear colorless fluid that is injected into the eye to hold the retina in place until it reattaches to the inner surface of the eye. We were told that it could stay in Jayla's eye for years.

Jayla did not like how she felt when she came out of her first-surgery, so she asked the anesthesiologist what other options were there. He told her that she could get the medicine through an IV instead of the mask. The intravenous route is the fastest way to deliver the medication to the body. She chose the IV and never looked back. She came out of this surgery not groggy, and feeling a lot better than before. The patch was put back on her right eye, and we resumed the round the clock eye drop regimen. However, she now had something new, an oil bubble in her eye, and our instructions were somewhat challenging for a child this age. We had to keep her head down for at least two weeks, no reading or watching TV. She could not lie on her back while she slept, so Jayla slept on me for two weeks. I wanted to make sure she did not roll on her back. We tried all kinds of things with her during this time of recovery, all the while trying to keep her spirits up. I found books on tape that I knew she would like, and I made up stories and told them to her all day and night. I knew God would give us what we needed when we needed it.

Jayla had been out of school for several weeks, and I knew that she would not be able to go back and finish the school year. She was in the third-grade, and I had to contact the school with our updated plans. I contacted our school counselor first and arranged for a meeting with her and Jayla's teacher. Once that date was set, we filled out all the necessary paperwork for Jayla to be on homebound instructions for the rest of the school year. To our delight, we were blessed with Ms. Lauren C., whom Jayla and I fell in love with upon our first meeting. She and Jayla would be together Mondays, Wednesdays, and Fridays for the allotted time. Jayla was excited to get back to some kind of routine.

I know that she was missing her friends from school and especially her dance friends. Jayla loved to dance and was just coming into her own style and was perfecting this art. I had to drive her sister Janai weekly back and forth to rehearsals, and every time I walked into the Dance Arts of Yardley studio, I would break down and cry. I knew I had to hold it together for Janai, so I cried only after she was in class. Everyone always asked about Jayla, and they all missed her very much. She was that special girl with a lot of sparkle. It broke my heart that even though she could not participate in the final dance recital, she wanted to attend to support her dance team. They did a special tribute to her at the recital, and we all were emotional. It pained me to see her so upset. Every time I made that drive from dancing school back home alone, I always cried for what my daughter Jayla lost. For many years, I had driven both girls back and forth, and the laughter we all had in the car was now gone. We were entering a new phase of life for Jayla and it was just the beginning of the pain she would endure.

Jayla's classes with Ms. Lauren were going fine, and she was so impressed with her. Jayla was determined to catch up and do her very best with the time she spent with Ms. Lauren. We continued with our Tuesday visits with Dr. Park at his Marlton New Jersey office, and Jayla was becoming a little superstar there. She was one of the youngest patients they saw, and everyone in the office looked forward to her arrival. She always made the other patients smile with her big personality and uncanny wit. Jayla was able to hold a conversation with everyone and had an opinion about everything.

I always knew when Jayla was not feeling well, it would be the only time she was quiet. It was Friday June 12, and she had complained about her head hurting. I asked her if she wanted me to cancel class with Ms. Lauren, and to my surprise she said, "yes," I knew then something was wrong. I asked her how bad the headache was and she said, "Mommy it hurts really bad" and from there she began to vomit. I grabbed her up quickly and headed to Wills Eye ER. I had a small bag next to her in the car just in case she vomited again. I wanted to cry, but instead I silently prayed as I looked at my baby and drove down Interstate 95 south, reassuring her that everything was going to be okay. We arrived safely and once again she was brought back immediately. They remembered Jayla from our first visit to the ER five weeks prior. She began to vomit again and I could see on the nurse's face her concern; she yelled for a doctor to come quickly. Once we cleaned Jayla up, the doctor was there. They took Jayla's eye pressure and to everyone's surprise it was a very high sixty. I knew I had to become an expert in all things relating to the retina. So the learning began and I started writing everything down in my journal.

My questions were:
1. How do you measure ones' eye pressure?
    They use an instrument called a Tono-Pen, which barely touches the eye's surface. Numbing drops are first placed onto the eye. Then, gently rests on the surface of the eye in order to get an accurate pressure reading.
2. What is a normal eye pressure?
    Normal intraocular pressures average between 12-22 mm Hg. The "mm Hg" refers to millimeters of mercury, which is a scale for recording the eye pressure.

They began to give her eye drops every fifteen-minutes to bring the pressure down. This process took several hours, and they were not going to let us leave until she was out of danger. Jayla's pressure came down to thirty-eight, and they were very confident that we would be able to continue her medication regimen at home. Once we were discharged from the ER, another appointment was scheduled as follow up on Tuesday June 16. That weekend Jayla was very tired and irritable, and I could see on her beautiful face that she was scared. She didn't understand all that was happening to her and the question that bothered her the most was, "How come I can't see?" She knew she had an operation to repair her retina, but it wasn't fixed at all; it actually is worse than we thought. As a mother, how does one explain to an innocent child that she might never get her sight back? I also had to help her not blame herself; Jayla kept saying, "Mommy, if I just went to bed instead of going to the bathroom to fix my hair, I would still have my eyesight." My beautiful little girl lamented over and over again. This was very hard for any mother to hear and to figure out how to answer those questions.

I had a good cry and let out all that was bottled up inside of me since the accident. Crying was my therapy and catharsis. I also turned to the Bible for comfort and asked God for guidance. My words were the same "Lord, no matter what the outcome, she belongs to you." Once I released all control and allowed God to be God, I felt comfort and at peace. I had to be strong for Jayla during this process; I knew she, as well as everyone else, was watching my every move.

At our next appointment, we learned that Jayla's eye pressure had dropped to twenty-eight, and we were heading in the right direction. Jayla was put on antibiotic and steroid eye drops daily and when other complications occurred, there were drops for that as well. I had become very comfortable with putting the eye drops in her eyes, and she wanted only me to do them. I had taught Janai how to administer them as well, I needed her to know just in case of an emergency. Janai was my helper, and I reminded her that she used to give

Jayla her nebulizing treatments when she was very young. As the big sister, Janai wanted to help in any way she could. I was trying to do my very best, as I was reminded of my very last conversation with my mother.

Jayla's accident affected us all, especially Carvon. He was the protector of our family, and his baby girl was hurting. His inability to fix this problem bothered him the most. He was very stressed at work, and now our family was experiencing a life altering accident. That evening I looked at him and saw something that I hadn't seen in him, FEAR. He wasn't sleeping, his behavior was changing and I began to get concerned about my husband's health and mental state.

It was the last week of school for the girls and usually an exciting time in the Johnsons' household, but this year everyone seemed to have lost their joy. I asked God to help me so that I could help them. The last day of school on June 18, 2009, Carvon came home asking for help. He had seen his doctor and was given something to help him sleep. I monitored him all weekend, and on Monday he called out sick, so I knew he wasn't well. For as long as I had known him, he had never called out sick. I knew this was serious and by Wednesday we were in the ER from a bad reaction from his medication. He was then given a complete medical examination and was sent home with new medication and a doctor's note.

On June 30, 2009, I began the process of short-term disability for Carvon, who was now battling severe depression. The summer of 2009 was one I will never forget. I had three loved ones home depending on me for everything. I started a medical binder for Carvon and Jayla and put all medical documents in them. I spent many hours organizing these binders and began to take them with me to all appointments. My calendar was filled with doctors and hospital appointments for them both. Again, I was asking God for strength, guidance and patience, to help me get through this medical journey.

Jayla continued to see Dr. Park every two weeks for her regular appointments to check her eye pressure and the condition of the oil bubble. The pressure had come down to a comfortable fifteen, and she was doing well so far that summer. We had the same wonderful teacher, Ms. Lauren, who worked with her over the summer, anticipating Jayla's return to school in the fall.

Janai had finished middle school and would be starting high school, and I was very concerned about her. Janai had watched me grieve over my mother, grandmother and other loved ones as she was grieving for them too. She was with her sister that Friday night when the hair clip broke and often wished that night never happened. Janai quietly holds all of her emotions inside and only a mother can quietly see them. She was hurting inside for her baby sister and her father, and I knew that she was broken-hearted over both of them. I prayed for Janai asking God to show me what I needed to do for her as her mother. God would always remind me that she belongs to Him and for me to love her and model for her "Strength through the Storms" and in this case, "Strength Through the Summer of 2009."

August 20, 2009, Jayla was scheduled for her third-surgery; her eye was rejecting the oil bubble. Dr. Park was going in and removing the oil and replacing it with a different kind of oil. This particular procedure was done at another location, the Main Line Surgical Center in Bala Cynwyd, Pennsylvania. My life friend and sister Damita met me there because she knew, I needed her. While we were there in the waiting room, Jayla started a conversation with a patient named Scott. He, too, was there because of a Retinal Detachment and was having his sixth-surgery. I was so amazed at their conversation

41

and how mature Jayla was in asking him about his eye surgeries. He and Jayla had something in common and were able to communicate how they felt about their injuries. We immediately connected with his wife and became instant friends. I felt blessed to have met such a caring and loving couple. We kept in contact, and they began praying for Jayla from that moment on. Scott went on to write a book, and he mentioned Jayla and how they met on that beautiful day. One never knows who God is going to put in one's path as they journey through life.

Jayla came out of the surgery well and was put back on several eye drops per day. It was a rough summer and not what we had expected. Jayla could not do any of the activities she was used to doing; such as swimming, bike riding, jumping rope, and her favorite, dancing. We also could not drive for long distances or fly anywhere. Our summer vacations were put on hold as well as our lives, but I knew it was all for a higher purpose.

That summer of 2009, we were homebound and she was starting to feel like her life was never going to be the same. I knew I had to be the one to let her know she was going to be fine and that God was in control. Jayla was sticking closely to me and would not allow me to leave her. I joked with friends and said if she could get back in my womb she would. There were days I wanted to just stay in bed and cry, or crawl up in a corner and hide from everyone. I couldn't do either, so I continued to get up every day and do my same routine.

The summer was coming to an end and the first day of school was August 31, Janai was very excited about starting high school and Jayla was going into the fourth-grade. After Jayla's third-surgery, Dr. Park and I decided that it would be best that Jayla remain home while she was healing from her surgery. So that meant she could not start on the first day, and she was not happy about this decision. Jayla was missing all of her friends, and I knew this was not what she wanted to hear.

On September 1, we went to our regular Tuesday appointment, and Dr. Park's face showed concern. By now I could sense when something was wrong. After the exam, he informed me that the retina had detached once again, and once again, he had to repair it. Jayla was scheduled for her fourth-surgery on September 22. How was I going to tell my baby that she would have to do this all over again so soon after her last surgery? This was now affecting us all, emotionally, physically and mentally, but no one more than Jayla.

I had to stay prayed up and in a positive mental state or I was going to lose it! Carvon was battling with his depression and could not return to work, Jayla was blind in her right eye and homebound, and my beautiful Janai was hurting and in pain as she watched her family struggle through this. I saw how frightened she became, and I made sure I told her everyday that I loved her, and that God will get us through this journey. I did not want Janai to feel that I did not see or understand how she was feeling. Her feelings were important to me, and I made sure that I spent quality time with her away from Carvon and Jayla.

As the girls were growing up, it was very important to me to spend time alone with them. We called it our heart-to-heart with Mommy. It could be a restaurant, movie, starbucks, our patio, their bedroom, or any place they wanted to go. It always turned out special for just us. I remember my prayer to God, when I was pregnant with Jayla, "Please give me enough love for them both" and God gave me enough for them all. This was a life lesson on overcoming no matter what is thrown in your path. I only prayed that my own mother could have wrapped her arms around me and whispered the same words that I told my daughters, "It's going to be okay." I missed her, but I knew she was watching over me.

The day of surgery went like all the rest, check in at the front desk and wait for them to call our names. The medical staff all knew Jayla by face and always made her feel very special when they saw her. Once her name was called, we entered the surgical suite and got into her blue gown, awaiting the nurse and the anesthesiologist. We had been getting the same team so they knew she was coming, and they were ready for her. They knew she preferred to be sedated by IV rather than the mask. All the doctors and nurses were so amazed at her strength and her positive outlook. Many shared with me that no child should have to go through all of these challenges at such a young age. Once she was all ready to go into surgery, I would stand over her and pray and tell her to go to her happy place and God would be there with her. The staff knew my ritual and always waited for me to finish. As soon as she was away from me, I broke down and cried and they knew this was also part of my ritual.

In recovery I was always able to look at my baby girl and give her the strength she needed and looked for after each surgery. Jayla was sent home with eye drops and more follow up. I had spoken to the administrators at Jayla's elementary school Sol Feinstone, and we had her all set up for homebound with her same instructor Ms. Lauren. Jayla was very happy about having Ms. Lauren come every day and work with her, she thought it was like being a superstar with her private tutor.

Once the eye patch was finally removed, Jayla had to start wearing glasses to protect the injured eye and to protect her seeing eye. If anything happen to Jayla's left eye, she would be completely blind. Of course, she selected frames that were very chic. They looked cute on her and all of her classmates were very kind when they saw her for the very first time with her new glasses. I tried to take Jayla in to see her classmates weekly.

Jayla's bi-weekly visits to Marlton, New Jersey continued for check-ups through the fall of 2009. Jayla continued to be busy during the day with homebound school work, and once school ended for the day, the two of us would go to watch Janai's volleyballs games. I knew that Jayla loved getting out of the house and supporting her sister with her activities. Carvon was not able to attend her games, and I knew that hurt her very much. Carvon was always leaving work early to watch his girls play volleyball and softball. It was very hard for Janai not seeing her Dad cheer her on from the stands.

Janai and Jayla were also involved with the Bucks County Chapter of Jack and Jill of America, Incorporated and Bucks County Chapter of the Links, Incorporated youth council and our church youth group. These girls kept me busy, there were days that I had been to two different hospitals and got home just in time for one of their activities. I had to keep them busy and maintain some kind of normalcy, because our home once filled with love, laughter and security, was now filled with heavy sadness and uncertainty.

In November Dr. Park noticed scar tissue building up around the eye from all of the surgeries. We knew that this buildup could occur again. It became worse, and on November 19, one week before Thanksgiving, Jayla was scheduled for her fifth-surgery. There are no words to describe how we all were feeling, we just did what had to be done. Through it all I was learning many things about my youngest child; she was teaching us all Ephesians 3:20 "Now unto him that is able to do

45

exceeding abundantly above all that we ask or think according to the power that worketh in us."

We celebrated Thanksgiving that year as we have done every year with Damita and Wayne along with other family and friends. We were so grateful and appreciative of everything that God had done in all of our lives. I knew that Jayla had a special gift and that God had a plan and purpose for her life. We just did not know what it was just yet, but it was forming.

Dr. Park and I agreed that Jayla should continue on homebound schooling for the remainder of the school year for her safety. Jayla loved this idea, and I began to think of creative ways we could expand her school day. My thoughts were we could have Jayla skype with her class during the day and have homebound lessons with Ms. Lauren while the students were in their specials, such as music, art, gym, etc. This was a new concept and not done before, but I was up for the challenge. I made several phone calls to the school's administration office with my request. My request was granted, and all was set up for her to begin to skype with her fourth-grade classmates at Sol Feinstone Elementary School.

This arrangement was very exciting for her and the other students. Jayla would start her day off sitting in our home office on the computer, in her pajama bottoms and slippers. They could only see the top of her, and she thought this was very funny, wearing pajamas to class everyday. I was very grateful to the Council Rock School District for accommodating Jayla and making it an easy transition. Let's just say after I finished advocating for Jayla, all things worked out in our favor. A mother has to do what a mother has to do, and this momma does not accept no as an answer!

I was on a serious mission to warn others about hair clip safety. I contacted all the media channels about

Jayla's story and was hoping someone would get back to us. To my surprise that week our local NBC channel 10 not only contacted us, but sent a reporter and camera crew to interview Jayla on February 10, 2010. The interview took place in our family room and Jayla was so excited and very articulate for a nine-year-old. She spoke about the injury, her five-surgeries and how much she loved having homebound instructions and skyping. She also warned everyone of the dangers of these hairclips and showed other products that are safer for girls to wear in their hair.

After the segment aired for all to see, the station received numerous emails wanting to know more about this little brave girl and their concerns about eye safety. Channel 10 sent us all the emails, and we answered every one of them. We found out that these hairclips injured other young women, and we were able to hear their stories. The segment was rebroadcast later in the week, with a doctor speaking about eye safety and eye care, answering many questions from viewers. Wow!, I was really impressed with the segment and thought it could turn into something more with Jayla being the spokesperson.

I did contact our attorney Bernard to see if we could take legal actions against the manufacturing company of the hair clip, but unfortunately we could not pursue any further. It seems that in order to pursue a class action lawsuit against such company you have to have the product, and Jayla threw the hairclip away when it broke. At the time, we never thought it would turn out like this, or we would have retrieved it from the trash. Many people asked me if we were angry, and I said the same thing I said from the beginning, no matter the outcome "God is in Control." I continued to Trust and believe in all of God's promises for our family.

Jayla was starting to get a lot of attention from the segment and our very good friend Wayne, put it on "Youtube" for all to see. Jayla was making a difference, and it was just the beginning. She was requested to speak on many occasions about her injury, and she had a story to tell. All of Jayla's friends were so supportive of her and loved that she was getting all of this attention, but no one was happier than her friend Brett Hoffman, Donna's son. Our young Brett in his spare time is a jewelry designer, and he decided to create a custom design and collection just for Jayla called "Hearts for Jayla." His idea came soon after Jayla was injured, and he wanted to do something special just for her and support Wills Eye Hospital. Brett went on to have several jewelry demonstrations and a percentage went to Wills Eye in honor of Jayla. I was so amazed by this remarkable young entrepreneur.

Our local newspaper got hold of this story and the two of them have been featured several times. I knew that Wills Eye needed to hear about this young man, so I took a copy of the article and met with the CEO of Wills Eye, Joe Bilson. Let me explain how I met him. I had an appointment with my husband downtown at Jefferson Hospital in June, and something told me to bring the newspaper article about Jayla and Brett. I remember grabbing the article and stuffing it in my briefcase. After Carvon's doctor appointment, I walked across the street to Wills Eye, walked into the lobby and looked in the directory for the administration department. Of course, it was on the top floor. I told Carvon to wait for me in the lobby. I pushed for the elevator, and up I went to meet the executive director of Wills Eye Institute.

I walked into a beautifully decorated office and met with the receptionist, who greeted me as I introduced myself and proceeded to tell her our story. She was so impressed and asked if she could make a copy and as soon as she walked away, I saw Mr. Bilson walking out of his office coming towards me. We were then properly introduced and immediately connected. He read the story and was impressed as well, by both Jayla and Brett. What happened next surprised even me. They called their chief development officer of foundations, Lauren. We walked to Lauren's office, and I told her all about Jayla's surgeries, Brett's compassion for her, and my reason for visiting. Needless to say, she was amazed and very interested. They all wanted to meet this young girl with all of this strength. A meeting was set for June 28, my birthday. Jayla was to meet with some of the other executives and physicians.

I was very excited for Jayla, and knew this was just the kind of involvement she needed. I shared all of this with Carvon, and he could not believe all of this transpired from an impromptu meeting. I just did what God told me to do and that was trust. The scripture that came to mind was Philippians 4:13, "I can do all things through Christ which strengtheneth me."

Jayla was dressed in her business attire and even carried a small briefcase to the first of many boardroom meetings at Wills Eye Institute. The same receptionist greeted us as we entered the fifteenth-floor of the executive suite. Jayla was then escorted to their boardroom filled with snacks just for her. She looked around at all the goodies and asked, "How many people are coming?" Lauren laughed and said everyone is coming to hear your remarkable story. That morning Jayla met with several people, including Dr. Alex Levin, Dr. Julia Haller and of course Joe Bilson CEO. Our little girl gave a performance that could have won her the Oscar. She was amazingly poised as she shared her story from the beginning and talked about how she wanted to help other children who have gone through similar experiences. Jayla wanted them to hear her perspective as a child, because she felt as though the experience in the hospital was not child friendly. She gave suggestions that they took into consideration, a child friendly video about eye surgery. The patient would view this video before and after surgery and see a child speaking to them. She also wanted the children to have a teddy bear and really cute pajamas, that was extra she said. At the time, in-patient surgery was done at Jefferson Hospital and their pediatric floor was really boring to her. She complained about the color on the walls, and the lack of books and games they had for the children, they were all outdated and needed new ones. She was told that many of the children don't stay for any length of time after their surgery, but they would take all she said into consideration and share with others.

We left that powerful meeting that day with a sense of accomplishment, hope and the birth of our non profit "Hearts for Jayla Foundation." What started as a kind gesture from Brett Hoffman was now supporting the community outreach programs and ophthalmic care and education for children in the Delaware Valley and surrounding suburban communities.

Our excitement continued that week as we were on our way to our first vacation since the 2009 accident. We traveled with our dear friends the Hoffman's, Steven, Donna, Brett and Anna, to Hilton Head South Carolina, what an awesome time we all had.

Once we returned from vacation, I had received a letter from Mid Atlantic Retina regarding our insurance company Aetna. The letter informed me that Mid Atlantic Retina had been working very diligently to arrive at a mutually acceptable contract with Aetna. After much discussion, they had decided to terminate their relationship with Aetna and were making every effort to reach an agreeable solution prior to the deadline of July 16, 2010. This concerned me because Jayla was scheduled for her sixth-surgery on July 14. It went on to say that Mid Atlantic Retina would remain an in-network provider during these discussions. I went on to read more and on the last page was a request for our assistance in making Aetna aware of the high quality care received at Mid Atlantic Retina, how Aetna's policies would affect our ability to receive this quality care, and the importance of maintaining Wills Eye Physicians as in-network providers.

A contact number was provided to register our feedback. After receiving this letter, I quickly called Mid Atlantic Retina for clarification and spoke with their business manager. I was surprised to find out that over 14,000 patients would be affected by this decision, but at the time my only concern was my daughter Jayla. I quickly looked up everything about Aetna and searched for their executive biographies and their mission and value statements. I called the corporate headquarters and the network provider representative daily for three weeks, leaving the same message, my name, Jayla's name, her condition and the quality of care from Mid Atlantic Physicians, and I always ended the call with my signature farewell, "Have a Blessed Day."

On July 8, I received another letter from Mid Atlantic Retina explaining that after months of negotiating, it now appears likely that a new contractual arrangement with Aetna will not be possible prior to the July 16, deadline. If you choose to continue your care with Mid Atlantic Retina, you will be required to pay all outstanding deductibles and applicable co-insurance amounts, per your benefit plan, at the time of service. Under the circumstances, some patients may choose to transfer their care to an Aetna participating physician. I was not about to transfer Jayla's care to another physician midpoint on and was very upset about this decision. Jayla was covered for her upcoming surgery on July 14, because it was before the deadline date of July 16. Dr. Park, Mid Atlantic Retina, and Wills Eye assured us that they would do everything possible to continue Jayla's care with them.

An executive from Aetna soon returned my call and was very curious about how I was able to reach him. If anyone knows me they will tell you, I am very persistent and I am always up for a challenge. He then surprised me with the name of a case manager that covered our area. Heather and I connected and worked very well together. Within a two-week time frame a Negotiated Letter of Agreement Between Aetna Health Inc. and Mid Atlantic Retina, regarding Jayla Johnson (The Member) was sent Priority Mail, and the contents were astounding. Aetna put a contract together for Jayla Johnson to continue to receive all services.

I received a call from Mid Atlantic Retina asking me what I did, and if they could hire me to negotiate their future contracts. Nice gesture, I thought, and I sent the involved parties a nice thank you letter. Once again, I was thanking God for the courage to press on, even when it looked like it was impossible.

On July 14, 2010, Jayla had her sixth-surgery to remove scar tissue. The routine was the same, and by now Jayla was a pro. The concern this time was her very low eye pressure, which had gone as low as a five. We had to monitor her pressure and hope that it would remain in a comfortable range. I knew Dr. Park was concerned because Jayla was scheduled to return to school in September.

Jayla had spent the last twelve-months homebound and I knew for her well being she needed to get back into the classroom full time. If Jayla was going to survive this trauma, she would have to overcome any fears she might have had and her dependence on me. I too, had to let my daughter be free to fall and fail in order to find her strength and voice to overcome the impossible.

Jayla bounced back from this procedure well and was looking forward to going back to school, but she was more excited about Lauren's wedding. Lauren had worked well with Jayla those twelve months and was very committed to her and her success as a student. The two of them had a special bond, and I knew Jayla was grateful for the dedication she had shown to her. Lauren and her family were now part of our family, and Jayla was asked to read a scripture in their wedding. It was so funny how many people knew all about Jayla and had been praying for her. Our little girl captured the hearts of many during this journey and only God knows the plans he has for her.

As that summer drew to an end, Dr. Park and I had many discussions over Jayla's schedule and spoke about her safety while she would be at school all day. Dr. Park was a very sensitive man when it came to Jayla and her eye care. We developed a strong relationship with him during this time and I trusted his judgment. We decided that I would drive Jayla to and from school because of risks associated with being jolted or hit on the bus. She was also to refrain from gym or any contact sports with any kind of balls and sticks.

I had been speaking with our school's instructional coordinator Linda over that summer, and we had put in place a 504 for Jayla for her return. This "504 plan" refers to Section 504 of the Rehabilitation Act and the Americans with Disabilities Act, which specifies that no one with a disability can be excluded from participating in federally funded programs or activities, including elementary, secondary or postsecondary schooling. "Disability" in this context refers to a "physical impairment." A 504 plan spells out the modifications and accommodations that will be needed for these students to have an opportunity to perform at the same level as their peers.

On August 30, 2010, Jayla now a fifth-grader, started back to school at Sol Feinstone Elementary School in Upper Makefield, Pa. for the first time since the May 2009 accident. I had met with the principal Mr. Harlan, and he and I went through the classrooms looking for anything that could possibly harm Jayla and her fragile eye. I felt safe knowing that she had to wear glasses for protection and knew what to avoid.

Jayla was looking forward to seeing all of her friends. She received a warm welcome by all the children, staff, and the principal. It didn't take long for our girl to get back into her routine. Jayla was always popular and had no problem making friends. Many of the students knew about her accident, but still had no idea all that she went through. Jayla looked the same to them except for her new glasses, and they were not your normal fifth-grade glasses. They were Vogue and fabulous eyewear that only Jayla could wear.

The first day I went in with her and stayed for just a while as she got adjusted. I spent time speaking with the school nurse Dana about her schedule for eye drops that had to be given four times during the school day. I acted like a new mother sending her child off to school for the very first time. My phone wrang off the hook from everyone asking how her first day went.

Jayla was happy to be back at school and eased her way into her routine. I told her to take each day as the beginning of a beautiful journey that God had planned just for her, and she did just that. Jayla made new friends and all the teachers loved her knowing all that she had gone through. She was our little celebrity from the news media, local newspapers, and magazine articles, all calling her courageous and unstoppable. Jayla took all of this adoration in stride and never once acted any differently. I continued to be amazed at this child and her capacity to make the best of any situation.

The next couple of months were going well for both my girls. Janai was now a sophomore at Council Rock North and Jayla continued to make great progress navigating back into school and her other activities. We were all so proud of our Jayla when she did a presentation in October to her Bucks County Jack and Jill group entitled, "Through Jayla's Eyes." It was all about eye care and fun facts. She put the entire program together with the help from Wills Eye, her sister Janai and her own research. We put an interactive package together for the kids to read and discuss with their parents. Jayla had the kids put an eye patch over their right eyes to get the feel of how she now saw the world. They were asked to do simple tasks, and some had difficulties performing them with their eye covered. Jayla also shared with the group the anatomy of the eye, and went over every part and its definition. I think they were very impressed and thought this was one of their favorite activities.

Jayla went on to do this same activity for her fifth-grade class. The proud mother shared this with Wills Eye, Dr. Park, and his entire staff. Everyone was proud of Jayla and spoke about this activity to share with other groups within their network.

We continued with our regular bi-weekly Tuesday appointments with Dr. Park to check the eye pressure and the condition of the oil bubble. In December, I noticed Jayla's eye was very red, and there appeared to be blood in her eye. We were scheduled to see Dr. Park on December 7, and I had all confidence that he would identify the problem. Dr. Park immediately knew after examining Jayla that she had what is called a hyphema. This condition was new for us, but it did not require surgery at the moment. A hyphema is blood in the front anterior chamber of the eye. It may appear as a reddish tinge, or it may appear as a small pool of blood at the bottom of the iris or in the cornea. It is frequently caused by injury and may partially or completely block vision. Dr. Park was concerned, and he was monitoring this condition and wanted to see Jayla weekly with the hope it would resolve on its own. The end of December, Jayla's eye healed nicely and the hyphema had resolved.

Jayla continued adjusting well in school and rarely complained about her injured eye. It is amazing how children are as resilient as they are after any type of trauma. Don't get me wrong, she had many moments when she would ask why the accident happened and expressed that she missed seeing out of her right eye.

As a mother, these were the moments I cried on the inside as I allowed her to show all of her emotions. I told Jayla that crying was a way of cleansing your soul, and it would make her feel better if she let it all out and never held anything in.

Janai was always there to support her sister, and they were developing a strong sisterly bond. Everyone at school was very protective of Jayla, especially her fifth-grade class. Her teacher Mr. Morecz was wonderful with Jayla that year and made the transition very easy. Jayla had to leave the classroom at least four times during the day for her eye drops, and Mr. Morecz assigned a timekeeper for Jayla to remind her when it was time to go to the nurse. The children took pride in this new classroom duty.

Jayla's eye pressure was still very low, and we were doing everything to get it back up to a normal range. I wasn't sure if it was because she was back at school and reading much more than before. Jayla was working so hard to keep up with her academics and all the demands of a fifth-grader. I would have to put a time limit on how long she would study and read her textbooks. Her eye was always so very red and looked like it was closed.

We continued our bi-weekly office visits seeing Dr. Park and on February 8, 2011, Jayla received an injection of steroids in her eye. The right eye was numbed and the nurse covered her left seeing eye so that she could not see the large needle that would be injected into her right eye. I held my daughter's hand and cried quietly as this procedure took place. She was in so much pain, and I prayed asking God to bring relief to our baby. She was going through so much, and I didn't know what else to do, but pray.

I had my own routine when we were at Jayla's appointments. We check in and I would talk to the wonderful staff, then Jayla was called into the vision room where they checked her pressure. We then went to another waiting room to be called into the exam room. Once there she was seated in the chair awaiting Dr. Park and the nurse. I sat in my chair and began to pray for a positive report. Dr. Park then comes in and greets us both and proceeds with the examination. I am praying the entire time until he turns from his chair and says, "Everything looks good." We schedule our next appointment and off we go back to school. Jayla's appointments are always at 8:30 am so I can get her back to school by 11:30 am. We have been doing this since May 2009, my car could drive itself to Marlton, New Jersey.

I kept Jayla home after this procedure because once the numbing wore off, she would be in a lot of pain. Her eye had a patch on it, and I was to take it off the next day. We were going to see if wearing the patch would increase the eye pressure. Janai was always around to help me with Jayla and remind me of her eye drops and other medications. Jayla could not swallow pills, so I had to ask for all medication to be in liquid form.

The Staff at Jayla's elementary school decided that they wanted to support Jayla's Foundation, so they came up with "Casual Day for a Cause." The funds raised would be donated to Wills Eye. The local paper came out and interviewed Jayla and her teacher Mr. Morecz. This was a fun day for the teachers to dress very comfortably. Jayla was quoted as saying, "knowing that the majority of the teachers are dressing down for my cause is pretty cool." In honor of Jayla the teachers made a nice donation to Wills Eye Hospital and we were very touched by this act of kindness and many others throughout our Bucks County community.

Jayla was becoming very comfortable back at school, and I knew she missed all of her activities, especially dance. Dr. Park told Jayla she could do ballet, but Jayla liked hip hop and jazz. She asked him every visit what kind of activity could she participate in. She was limited in what she could do, but that never stopped her for pushing for the things she wanted to do. Dr. Park always had lively conversations with her and I enjoyed their debates back and forth. Jayla was determined to win him over one day.

On Wednesday April 13, 2011, Jayla was having her seventh-surgery to remove the oil bubble and repair the pupil. Here we go again, it had been calm for awhile since Jayla's last surgery. We checked into admissions at Wills Eye Hospital and were greeted with a smile from the receptionist. They all knew Jayla and her story and really did not like seeing her here under these conditions. I must say Jayla was always treated special, I never had any complaints about the care she received from the medical staff or their facilities. Most of the more complicated surgeries were done at this location, and we knew what to expect. Jayla stayed home the rest of that week and recovered comfortably and once again my heart was breaking for my baby. I often wondered about her emotional capacity to endure all these surgeries as well as the mental and physical impact it was having on her young life.

Many people started questioning me about the surgeries since she still had no vision. I could only say "Miracles do happen" and "I believed and trusted God for the outcome." Dr. Park was trying to do everything possible to keep Jayla's eye viable and intact. I asked God to show me in his word something that would help me understand this journey. I was led to Genesis 50:20 "you intended to harm me, but God intended it all for good. He brought me to this position so I could save the lives of many people" and verse 21, "No, don't be afraid. I will continue to take care of you and your children, so he reassured them by speaking kindly to them." when I read this verse I felt comfort and peace. I looked at all that God was doing in Jayla's life, and the many people she was touching through this journey.

Jayla returned back to school and was welcomed very warmly from her classmates and teachers once again. They too, were wondering how much more she could take. We were all watching for signs of any personality changes or anything that was out of character for Jayla. I think the teachers were amazed that she continued to be the outgoing little girl she always was. Nobody was watching her more than I was, and nobody knew her better than I.

Jayla and I have a very strong mother-daughter bond, and it was strengthened during this journey. I allowed Jayla to express her feelings and told her that she did not have to be strong all the time. I did not treat her like she was disabled or allowed anyone else to treat her differently. I always told Jayla that God has a plan and purpose for her life, and Mommy and Daddy were trusting God to see her through. Jayla was able to see for herself all that God was doing for her and our entire family.

It was not easy on my girls as they were witnessing their father slip deeper and deeper into his depression, they were afraid for him, for us. They were young and did not understand how this could happen to such a strong man who always protected them, provided for them, and loved them. Carvon became someone they didn't know or recognize, but I knew he would come out of this, it was just a matter of time.

In June of 2011, Janai was part of the Future Faces of Wall Street, and the group visited the NYSE where they had the opportunity to ring the closing bell. This trip was in conjunction with the Delaware Valley Chapters of Jack and Jill of America and the Bucks County Chapter of the Links Incorporated and was one of many highlights of her life. I was honored to have been there to witness this day with her. Janai completed her sophomore year with honors, and Jayla made it through the fifth-grade and was looking forward to her last year in elementary school. That year was trying for our family, a family that looked perfect from the outside, but was very broken on the inside. I refused to look like my circumstances and continued to trust and believe in all of God's promises for our family.

Storms have to end, but ours seemed to continue and pick up intensity every year. Many did not know how serious Carvon's depression was, and only a very few knew the truth. I felt like I was losing my husband, as he continued his battle, and I knew I could not save him. We spent hours sitting together praying, reading, and listening to music. I tried motivating him with stories of the girls and how well they were doing in school and I kept him updated with all of their activities. I knew he was proud of our girls, but I could see and feel his pain as he was struggling just to get through the day. Carvon kept to himself and had little contact with them during this time. My husband was receiving the best medical treatments and therapy. I knew this battle was his to overcome, and I stayed by his side loving him and praying for that day to come.

We all were trying to survive day by day, especially Janai. I continued to have my concerns for our oldest daughter, who began struggling emotionally, and I knew she needed to talk to someone, besides me. There were days, too many to count, that I felt like I was drowning with everyone's problems. I would solve one and then get hit with twenty more. I became the captain of Team Johnson and told them every day that we were getting stronger, and that God was ordering our steps. Our Motto was: "Hold on, God got us, we don't quit, we keep moving forward!" I decided that everyone was going to therapy, self care for Team Johnson and I made appointments for us all.

My self care was Friday mornings at 10:00am at the hair salon, "T Monique's Hair Design," it was the only time I had to myself. Both girls were in school and Carvon was at therapy. It was my outing to be able to talk to friends that loved and supported me, my village. It became a ministry for me to share my story of faith and how God was sustaining our family. I would wake up early, make breakfast, drop everyone off, get my starbucks and head straight to the salon. The salon became my place of release where I was able to cry, laugh, and be a witness of what God was doing in my life. The women saw all of my trials and triumphs as if it were a real life drama unfolding right before their eyes. God allowed me to be transparent, and out of that came "Joyful Living." I have been told hearing my testimony has changed many lives in that salon. God will put people in your life for a reason and a season, but we must know that it's for His purpose and His glory.

Janai was entering her junior year with all the excitement of things to come. We were preparing for all the scholastic testing, essay writing, the financial aid and scholarship application process. She had narrowed down her college choices to her top five: Drexel University, University of Maryland, University of Pittsburgh, St. Joseph University, and West Chester. I was more excited about the wonderful opportunities for my daughter than she was. It was a mother's dream to be able to watch her daughter graduate from high school and go off to college. I remember how excited my own mother was for me. Janai was more focused than ever before and really wanted this to be a great year for her. Wonderful things were happening, and she was happy and filled with joy.

In November of that same year, our beautiful Janai participated in the Delaware Valley Rites of Passage, which prepares our teens from youth to adulthood. The program consisted of three phases, The Preparation, The Seperation and The Presentation. This process was a year-long, and Janai and I enjoyed every moment of it together.

I was thanking God for this opportunity of bonding with Janai. Every weekend she had some sort of activity pertaining to the Rites of Passage as they prepared for the Black and White Gala celebration. The whole family was looking forward to this grand affair, and we invited our family and friends to celebrate with us. A very good friend of the family, the Gilberts, gifted us the most beautiful white ball gown that had belonged to their beautiful and beloved daughter Taylor.

We had just celebrated Thanksgiving that year, and the Gala was to be held that Saturday. We were so thankful for all the blessings that we had received to get to this day. That Saturday morning all the Johnson girls went to get our hair and nails done for the gala. Janai looked at me and said, "Mommy, this is how it's going to be on my wedding day." I smiled and said, "Yes it is, and I am going to be this calm on that day too." We both laughed and cried at the same time. Believe it or not, I was very calm that day, and the girls never knew what I had to do to pull this all together. I prayed for peace, strength and patience and God gave me all of them.

Carvon was not himself that morning and I did not know what to expect from him. My only concern that day was, I had to make this a beautiful experience for Janai the best way I knew how. She looked like a princess, so beautiful and graceful, as she was presented to the village. During that night the fathers and their daughters danced a beautiful waltz; it brought tears to my eyes as I watched Janai and Carvon on that dance floor. I knew that Carvon missed his little girl and wanted to heal their relationship, but he had to heal himself first. In that brief moment; I saw a very loving and caring father with his beautiful daughter in his arms dancing, something I never experienced with my own father. I think all little girls dream about their wedding day; and having their father walk them down the aisle and that first father-daughter dance. I thank God that I had my grandfather, my Pop Pop with me on my special day. I was so proud of Janai that night, because I, better than anyone, knew all that she had been through to get to that moment. That night I saw my daughter as the young woman she was to become. I look back at that beautiful evening and wish that my mother could have been there to see how beautiful the girls looked all dressed up. Our family portrait of that night is proudly displayed in our foyer for all to see. No one knew the pain I was feeling as I took that picture. My family was broken, hurting and only God could fix and heal us.

Janai felt really good about herself after that experience, and it was just what she needed to keep her spirits up. As 2011 was coming to an end, I sat down and reflected on all that had happened to our family and all I could say was, "Thank you God for keeping us all together." I was also thanking God for our inner circle of prayer warriors that surrounded us each and every day with prayers, love, and support. They were the only ones who knew about Carvon. God clearly had told me that Carvon's testimony was his to share, and when he was ready, he would have the opportunity.

Many days, I talked to God about Carvon, always ending with the refrain, "Lord please heal my husband." Everyone asked me what I wanted, and my answer would always be the same, "Joy." I knew if I kept joy in my heart, I would be able to get through anything. In the face of so many life challenges many people would have just given up, but I had to press on until the end, and I was hoping the end was near.

The storms continued to intensify and in January 2012, we lost our health insurance. My husband's company discontinued our health care coverage, and he was still out on disability. My only concern was for Jayla, Janai and I were healthy and only saw our doctors for our yearly exams. I was praying we would not have any unexpected emergencies. Dr. Park was kind enough to continue seeing Jayla until we worked this insurance crisis out.

My life had taken on unanticipated challenges once again; my husband was home on long-term disability, we had no health insurance and my youngest daughter was blind in her right eye and required monthly visits to the doctor. What a humbling experience for anyone to face, I had never imagined I would be in this situation. We thought we had done everything right, only to find out, God had a different plan for our family. We went from two incomes and premium insurance to none, but we were still together in our home. It made no sense to man but all sense to God. We were getting blessings from everywhere, as I was trusting and believing in God to do all the rest. That was all I knew how to do.

Our last year at Sol Feinstone was bittersweet for all of us. We were saying goodbye to the school that both girls attended since first-grade. I was a very active Mom there and became friends with many of the teachers, administrators, and other parents. We were so honored when the Student Council decided to raise awareness about eye care and safety to honor Jayla and Wills Eye Institute by hosting *"Eye Awareness Day"* in the gym. The students and staff participated in an Interactive Eye Museum, which offered a variety of educational exhibits and games. The students were also able to watch Jayla's interview and meet with her to answer any questions. We received many thank you letters from parents and beautiful words of encouragement for Jayla. We were touched by everyone's commitment and the event's success.

That summer Jayla and Brett were asked to come and take pictures for Wills Eye Institute, to be published in their magazine. To everyone's surprise, Joe Bilson the CEO of Wills Eye, made his way into the pictures. It was a great day for these two young philanthropists. The magazine featured the picture of Brett, Jayla, and Joe and an informative article:

Nationwide, one out of every four children suffers from a serious disorder. In our area, more than 80 percent of children receive basic eye screening, but only two-thirds of Philadelphia children who fail the screening follow-up with needed care. This care, which ranges from ensuring a child receives eyeglasses to treatment for serious ophthalmic conditions, is necessary for reading, school performance, and normal cognitive development. The Wills Eye Pediatric Ophthalmology and Ocular Genetics Service understand the potentially devastating consequences of untreated vision disorders all too well. Will's commitment to helping children get eye care has been bolstered by two exceptionally creative, philanthropically minded young people. Three years ago, 8 year-old Jayla Johnson was partially blinded when a hair clip spring snapped and propelled a piece of metal into the right eye. The injury detached her retina and damaged her lens, requiring multiple surgeries. However, Jayla's positive outlook never wavered. To raise awareness of the importance of eye safety and the need for timely eye care, she and her family created the Hearts for Jayla Foundation, which raises money to support the Sight 4 Kids Campaign at Wills. Inspired by his friend's courage, Brett Hoffman, now thirteen, and CEO of his own jewelry company, BH Designs, LLC. Honored Jayla by creating the Hearts for Jayla jewelry collection. Jayla and Brett, kids helping kids, are powerful partners with a concern for others that is amazing at such a young age. "You can take something tragic, turn it around and make it a force for good which impacts so many lives," says Jayla's mother, Robyn Johnson. "And that's exactly what Brett and Jayla have done." The funds raised by Jayla and Brett support community outreach programs and ophthalmic care and education for children.

What a way to end that year at Sol Feinstone!.

That summer also represented an opportunity for Carvon to begin telling his story. We had not been on a family vacation since our trip to Hilton head in 2010 with the Hoffmans. This trip was with our family friends the Wilsons, and we were headed back to beautiful South Carolina, to visit Liz's parents on their farm. We all were looking forward to this much needed vacation.

That Saturday before we were to leave, Carvon spoke at our monthly men's breakfast at Christian Stronghold. It was his chance to share his story with everyone, especially all the men. Janai helped him with the title "3,2,1 Rebound-You Fall, Now Get Up!" I knew that speaking freely about his clinical depression was the beginning of his healing and an answered prayer. After his emotional and heartfelt testimony, many men came up to my husband seeking advise, love and help. Clinical depression is very treatable with the correct diagnosis, right medications, talk therapy and a great support system all working together.

That weekend was therapeutic for our family, and I was also thanking God for the opportunity to travel once again. We had a wonderful week with the Wilsons and even took a side trip to Charleston, South Carolina. I really should have been born in the South. I just love the hospitality, food and the beautiful scenery. I am a Carolina girl at heart and can't wait to get back there to visit or to live one day.

A Mother's Love for Janai

A miracle journey brought me back to joy.

We were all getting ready for the new school year as Janai was beginning her senior year and Jayla to begin middle school. As Jayla adjusted to changes at her new school, little did we know that Janai would soon confront a severe medical crisis of her own.

At this point in my girls' journey, I was thinking earnestly about Janai preparing for graduation in June 2013 and entering college. All of my dreams were coming true for our Janai. We had submitted all of her applications for college admission, scholarships, and financial aid. I kept believing and trusting in God for a financial blessing to help with Janai's tuition. How do you tell your daughter that all of our personal savings and her college funds have been used to support the family during the many trials we had experienced. I cried many nights thinking about our financial challenges.

Carvon and I never thought we would be in this predicament. We had lived our entire married life debt free, and here we were in debt for the very first time in our marriage. I did not like this feeling, and I knew my husband wasn't proud of the situation either. How were we going to pay for our daughter's college tuition? We were blessed that my husband had a natural gift for financial planning, so we never had to borrow from anyone, even though I was tempted to ask several times.

In addition to preparing for Janai to graduate and enter college, I still had another major dilemma that was weighing heavy on my heart, and that was health insurance for my children. I had received information about Chip (Children's Health Insurance Program) and left it for Carvon to investigate. That evening, December 10, 2012, God spoke to me and told me to fill out the application, so I filled it out and mailed it off. Again, I would have never thought we would be in this situation, but we were. I was thankful for the great relationships I had with Dr. Heather Lubell, Dr. Carl Park, and Dr. Chris Landes. They all knew what our family was going through and helped me out when I needed it the most. I will always be grateful for the kindness they showed our family during these trying medical times.

On January 14, 2013, I went to the mailbox and to my surprise, I received notification from CHIP that we were approved for insurance. However, they were requesting employment verification from Verizon, a place I never worked, so I knew this was an error. I immediately called to clarify, and Verizon asked me to document the error in a letter. After I hung up the phone, I knew God was up to something, and it was going to work in my favor, I sent the letter and waited. Around the same time, Janai had received her first acceptance letter to the University of Pittsburgh, and what a relief she felt. She had also received acceptances from West Chester and IUP, but of course she was hoping to get a letter from her number one school, Drexel University. I assured her that she had done everything she could do, and it was all going to work out in her favor, just believe and trust God.

Janai had a lot on her plate that year, and she had to manage her time wisely. She was the Teen President of Bucks County Jack and Jill and was preparing for the upcoming Teen Conference in Boston from March 21-24, 2013. Janai had been in Jack and Jill since she was seven years old, and every teen looked forward to the last Teen Conference when they graduate out of Jack and Jill. It is a beautiful ceremony for the seniors, their parents, and other teens to witness. The young ladies are dressed in white ball gowns and the young men in tuxedos. We all were looking forward to this special night, especially Janai.

The Bucks teens were busy getting ready for the conference, preparing for their Chapter's scrapbook, banner, and display. A lot of work goes into this conference every year, and the results are always amazing. Janai was very organized and was heading up the scrapbook committee, she wanted to get things started early. On Saturday, January 19, we went shopping for all the materials for the scrapbook and then went to the movies. We had a wonderful mother-daughter evening. The next day we attended church and Mr. Harper, Angel's father surprised us and we all worshipped together. It was a great service about overcoming trials and tribulations, what a message, and perfect timing!

That Monday was our Martin Luther King Day of service with Bucks County Jack and Jill and other organizations at Second Baptist Church of Doylestown, and we all attended. The girls enjoyed helping pack meals for the homeless, making quilts for the babies, and donating clothes and other essentials for Cradles for Crayons. It was such a great day of service for our community.

On Tuesday January 22, 2013, Janai woke up the same as she had done all through high school at 6:15 am, she showered, got dressed and went downstairs for breakfast. I remember her saying "Bye Mommy I love you" and I always responded, "I love you too and have a blessed day." I got Jayla up and drove her to school and when I returned I went to lie back down because of a migraine. I began to dream about Janai and in my dream I saw her in pain, running in the house crying. At that exact moment, I woke up after hearing the chimes from the back door and hearing Janai's voice screaming! I thought I was still dreaming until I heard her crying, I ran down the stairs, and what I saw broke my heart.

Janai was running around our family room crying and saying "Mommy, I want my joy back." "Mommy, I want my joy back please." I looked at Carvon and asked "what was going on, what happened?" He told me that Janai was in her business class and could not concentrate, so she asked if she could go to the nurse. She told the school nurse she wasn't feeling well and something felt different. She called my cell phone but I did not hear it ringing, so she called the home phone. Carvon answered and he knew immediately something was wrong with our daughter and went to get her. Once Janai saw him she fell into his arms not saying a word, just shaking and crying.

My initial thoughts were, that she was having a panic attack and we had to get her help immediately. I got dressed in fifteen-minutes talking the entire time to Carvon about where we needed to take Janai. I called my cousin Judy, who is a psychiatrist and explained what I was seeing and hearing with Janai. I then decided to take her to Abington Crisis Center, not knowing what to expect, I grabbed a notebook. When we arrived at the ER, Janai was seen quickly and the barrage of questions began about the state of mind of my daughter. I remembered answering everything honestly, but a nurse and social worker looked at all of us with doubt. These were very personal questions, and as I repeated myself over and over again, saying the same thing, "My child is not on drugs, something else is going on." The doctors, whom I began to refer to as "The White Coats," soon began the ordering of; a comprehensive metabolic panel, drug screen urine and serum, EKG and a CT scan of her brain.

After sitting there for hours, all the preliminary tests came back NEGATIVE. However, we were still waiting for a "White Coat" to come in and examine Janai, and by this time she was becoming very agitated. Someone sat outside her room monitoring her behavior, but I was becoming angry because no one had come in to check on my daughter. I told Carvon not to take his eyes off of Janai, while I walked around to the nurse's station as they all appeared to be standing around doing nothing. I began screaming, telling them that my daughter was sitting in an exam room in need of immediate medical attention! A male nurse then looked at me and said something very inappropriate that I ignored, but I gave him a look I know he will never forget!

After that intense interaction, two "White Coats" finally examined Janai and she was then given a small tablet of Ativan 1mg to calm her down. We sat and watched our daughter go through changes that we had never seen before. She began to have involuntary movements with her hands, slurred speech, and crying episodes, all with a blank stare on her face. I was crying on the inside and praying to God for healing, I was now concerned for my daughter's health.

We later met with a social worker regarding next steps in this medical journey. She gave us information on facilities that could evaluate Janai and give us a medical diagnosis. Three facilities were presented, and once again, I called my cousin Judy and Lisa, Damita's sister who is a psychiatric nurse. They both suggested the Horsham Clinic. I then called Wayne and Damita to keep them updated and they told us they would meet us there. Earlier that day, I had called our good friends Kathleen and Bill to get Jayla from school and let her stay with them until we knew what was going on. I knew Jayla would be comfortable with them, they were family and part of our Bucks County Village.

Before we left Abington, I had asked for all of Janai's medical reports from that day. I also asked the "White Coats" to explain to me what could be wrong with my daughter since her reports were all negative. They could not give me an answer and I was not satisfied not knowing. I then knew I had to get more information and was determined to find help for my daughter. My head was spinning and I was trying to keep it all together. I prayed to God for healing and strength as we were entering the Horsham Clinic. My first impression was not a good one, I knew I was not leaving my baby in this place. She did not belong there and I was ready to take her and run. It was a very dark and gloomy place and I held onto Janai with everything I had in me that night. I was not letting her go and she was not letting go of me.

There was no one at the front desk when we arrived that night, but within a few minutes a woman appeared to get our information. I was prepared with all the paper work I had collected from Abington, and handed her the inter-facility patient transfer form and medical reports to make copies. I wanted the "White Coat" seeing her to have all the updated information, hoping to avoid the same questions. Once all the information was taken, we were asked to go sit in the waiting room.

I took Janai in my arms, and with Carvon, we walked right into something I never want to see, ever again.

The large room was filled with so many children, all with their social workers, parents, and caregivers. The windows and television were all barred up, and there was nothing bright and cheery in that room. We took a seat along the wall, and Damita and Wayne were sitting next to us. I held Janai tightly in my arms as she repeated, "Mommy, please, don't leave me here."

We could hear everyone's conversations, and my heart was breaking for all of these beautiful children. One girl Janai's age was there because she had started a fight in her group home and locked her counselor in a room. She was sitting in front of us writing vigorously on her arms with a ballpoint pen and being very verbal to her social worker. I sat and watched this beautiful child act out her anger towards the world. I heard her repeatedly say "My Mom doesn't care what happens to me, you can call her if you want, but she isn't going to do anything, she can't handle me and that is why I am here." The social worker tried to talk to her and explain that everyone was trying to help her. I even tried to make eye contact with her so I could have given her a motherly smile. She turned to avoid looking at me, but that did not stop me from praying for her and the others in that dark and gloomy room.

When we were finally called to meet with the "White Coat", Dr. B. a psychiatrist walked in to greet us. I explained calmly what had occurred with Janai over the last couple of hours and she listened and was one of the few who heard me. She began to read over the medical reports from Abington Hospital and made her own notes. Dr. B. looked up and started to speak to Janai, asking her several questions about her life, her family, and what she thought was happening. Janai opened up and shared many things with her that night, especially about Carvon and the last four years of our family crisis. I held back my tears as she recounted Jayla's injury and her father's battle with depression. My daughter had been under a lot of stress, more than anyone ever knew, including me.

After that assessment was over, Dr. B. looked at me and said, "Your daughter does not belong here."She suspected Janai had been experiencing stress as a senior and the other pressures that we were having as a family. She did recommend that Janai begin to see a therapist. I was relieved, but something medically was still not right with my daughter. The doctor had given me names of some great adolescent therapists to call the next day. We thanked her and drove home that late evening feeling very grateful that our daughter was not spending the night in that facility. We picked Jayla up from Kathleen and Bill's and we were all together as a family, the beginning of another medical journey.

That night both girls slept in our bed, as Carvon and I held our daughters in our arms. I woke up very early that Wednesday morning, January 23, and began calling some of the therapists on the list. I wanted to get Janai an appointment as soon as possible. I was in Carvon's office on the phone when Janai appeared in the doorway, I looked up at her beautiful face and said, "Good morning sweetheart" and she smiled and said, "Good morning Mommy." I asked her how she was feeling and she said better. I explained to her what I was doing and offered to fix her breakfast. She said she wasn't hungry and just stared at me with a very peculiar look on her face. We weren't given a prescription for the Ativan, but in case she had any other outburst, I was told to give her Benadryl to keep her calm.

I began researching our options for an outpatient facility and found one in Doylestown, the Lenape Valley Foundation. They agreed to see Janai the next day because they accepted walk-ins on Thursdays. The rest of the day I spent making phone calls to friends in the medical community asking questions regarding Janai's condition. I was watching with a very careful eye, looking for any signs that would give me a clue to what was happening. I recorded what she ate, her behavior her speech and how long she slept. If something was not right, I was surely going to see it, and something was definitely wrong with my daughter. That evening I had Janai sleep with us once again, I wanted her near me. Of course, Jayla wanted to sleep with us as well. I did not get any sleep that night as I was watching over my daughter's every movement.

I am not Afraid of the "White Coats"

Can't think Clear when you reside in Fear.

On Thursday January 24, 2013, everyone woke up around 6:30 am, we ate breakfast together and Carvon drove Jayla to school. I had to help Janai get into the bathroom because she was acting very nervous and was upset. I ran a bath for her and helped her into the tub. As I was washing her back, she began to move around in the water and started speaking very fast, but I could not understand anything she was saying. I got her out of the tub, and she ran to her room crying. I was trying to dry her off, but she would not stay still. I managed somehow to get her underwear on and a pair of sweatpants and a loose-fitting top. As soon as Carvon walked through the door, he heard the commotion going on upstairs and ran to see what was happening. I said we have to leave now, something is terribly wrong.

We all got in the car that morning and began the twenty-five minute drive to Doylestown. Suddenly, Janai had another outburst of tears, and strange hand movements. I had to jump in the backseat to control her while Carvon continued driving. We drove up to Lenape, and I ran out to let someone know that Janai was very agitated and confused. I was instructed to take her next door to Doylestown Hospital Crisis Center, so we drove around to the Emergency entrance and Carvon dropped us at the door. I ran in holding Janai and quickly told them what had happened. We were immediately put in a room and seen by a nurse who took our information. Within fifteen-minutes, we met with a "White Coat", Dr. Kim, who I connected with right away. I told him Janai's medical history and gave him the medical reports from Abington Hospital and the report from the Horsham Clinic. He had asked if she was given any medication. I told him Ativan, the day, the time, and the strength. I had everything written down in a journal that I was now carrying with me. I shared with Dr. Kim the last couple of days since the onset of this bizarre behavior. What I loved most about him was that he listened and believed me when I said "this is not just mental, it's also medical." He then gave Janai Ativan 2mg at 10:15am, and he sat in the room with us as I began to figure out our next steps. I needed a plan, and I asked him where I could take my daughter to get the help she so needed. As I said that, I looked at him and said very determined "We are going to Children's Hospital of Philadelphia."

Janai was calming down at this point and I made sure I sat in the backseat with her as we drove to CHOP. We arrived at 12 noon, and went right to the ER, where we sat until our name was called. I was praying, asking God to heal my baby, begging actually. Please God, hear me and help us once again. We were finally escorted to a private room where a young and caring nurse began the process of gathering information of Janai's present illness, her physical examination, and her past medical history. I had given the nurse the most recent medical report from the last two days of our medical nightmare. This nurse had been very gentle with Janai and most understanding with me.

I recall several of the "White Coats" that afternoon coming in to see Janai from every department of medicine. The one that stands out the most and the one I will never forget is Dr. A., a female pediatric adolescent psychiatrist who was on call that day in the ER. She walked in, looked me up and down, had no bedside manners, was cold and condescending, especially to me. I was use to "White Coats" like this and was quite prepared for her. I spoke very calmly, looking her straight in the eyes as I repeated Janai's last couple of days. She then asked me about any drugs in her system and I assured her there were none except the Activan she was given. She looked at me as if I was lying to her. I then asked her if she read the most recent medical report from Abington Hospital that showed no drugs in Janai's system. She dismissed that information and never answered me and started examining Janai, and within five minutes she made a diagnosis that shocked me. This "White Coat" began to tell me that my daughter was having some sort of psychotic episode and needed immediate psychological help, and that I, her mother was in denial. I responded to this "White Coat" with sheer determination and the threat of legal action against her and this hospital if she did not admit my daughter immediately. Janai was soon admitted that early evening of January 24, 2013, as her mother had requested.

While we had been sitting in another waiting room, I knew I would have to verify our insurance. I explained to the representative that my daughter was in the ER, and getting ready to be admitted. I desperately needed our insurance retroactive to represent January 1. I knew God was working in our favor when I received that error, I just didn't know how. They processed the insurance and we were now awaiting a bed for Janai. It was around 10 pm and both of us were exhausted, hungry, scared and thinking about Jayla. I had earlier called our neighbors, Beth and Jay to get Jayla and let her stay the night with them. I knew the both of them along with their daughter Katie, would take good care of my baby while we were figuring this out. Also, I did not want Jayla to worry about her sister or to ask detailed questions to which we did not yet have the answers.

Next, we began to focus on getting our church family involved. Carvon had called Stronghold to get everyone praying for Janai and once that chain started, it was not going to stop. Carvon's phone started blowing up with prayers from friends and family. I kept busy keeping Janai calm and getting answers from the medical staff. Two nurses arrived and we were soon escorted to the fifth-floor of CHOP, the adolescent side of the floor. With the help from one of the nurse, we got Janai into a hospital gown and into her bed. The room was private and big enough for all of us to stay over that night. It didn't matter to me if it were the size of a tiny closet, this mother was not going anywhere. I sat beside her as the nurses took vitals and I began to write in my journal the names of every person who came in contact with Janai. After they left, Janai began crying and whispering something to me that I could not hear or understand. I had to lean in very closely as my daughter whispered, "Mommy, I don't want to die, please help me." I held my daughter tightly that night and whispered to her "you are not going to die, Mommy is here and so is God."

A young resident on call that night entered our room, sat down next to Janai, looked at me and listened. All "White Coats" are not the same, some really do believe in the Hippocratic Oath. Dr. Jona was one of the kindest and most compassionate physicians I had ever met. He had the best bedside manners and became the first "White Coat" to be on Team Johnson. Carvon was just outside of Janai's room on the phone, and Dr. Jona stepped outside as well, only Janai and I were in the room when it happened. Janai had her first seizure right in front of me, she had a generalized convulsion for 30 seconds or so. She bit the side of her tongue during the seizure, and blood was all over the front of her hospital gown. I screamed! for help, and I mean everyone heard me. The entire five-west medical team came running into Janai's room. It was like bells and whistles going off on the fifth-floor. I now have all of your attention, the problem now became a serious medical issue. They quickly gave her medication for the seizure and started cleaning her up, as I watched this medical nightmare begin to unfold right in front of everyone.

Many "White Coats" began to convened in our room to discuss what actions were to occur next. The first test they discussed with us was a "lumbar puncture", (LP) also called a "spinal tap" a procedure to collect and look at the fluid "cerebrospinal fluid", (CSF), surrounding the brain and spinal cord. During a (LP) a needle is carefully inserted into the spinal canal low in the back (lumbar area). Samples of a patient's (CSF) are collected and studied for color, blood cell counts, protein, glucose and other substances. Some of the samples may be put into a special culture cup to see if any infection, such as bacteria or fungi grows. If Janai had some sort of brain infection, this test would identify it quickly.

It was now after midnight, and Janai was still getting more blood work done. Then she had a second seizure, and everyone witnessed this one. Janai was becoming more and more agitated and very confused. I looked at my baby lying in that bed, and I saw all the life slowly being drained from her. She no longer looked like our Janai; my daughter was fading away before us and I did not know how to bring her back. Dr. Jona had the results of the spinal tap around 2:00 am, and told us that Janai indeed had a form of (encephalitis) an infection in her brain, but did not know what kind. I knew that more results would be coming later that morning. Janai was very tired, she was given medication to make her sleepy and that was what she needed; in fact, we all needed sleep. Janai's condition was very serious and I could not believe another medical crisis was happening to our family once again. Every human test possible was performed on our daughter, and all the results came back negative. This was now turning into a medical mystery.

Early the next morning Janai was set up for an "electroencephalography"-(EEG) a test that detects abnormalities in your brain waves. They also ordered more lab work on a child that did not sleep well and looked exhausted. It was around 7:00am that several "white coats" from different specialties began to come in and out of our room to examine Janai. I didn't get any sleep and was up and had already made several phone calls. I made sure Jayla was okay and spoke to her before she left for school and told her that we would see her later in the day. I tried to reassure her that Janai was fine but that the doctors wanted to run more tests on her before we could come home.

Outside of Janai's room I had noticed a group of five medical students, two men and three women from Neurology. I became curious and walked out of the room and introduced myself. To my surprise they were there to find out about Janai and her medical mystery. I then explained how we ended up at CHOP, and they were all fascinated to learn more of our medical nightmare. I mentioned the ER episode, and the "white coat" who did not believe me and did not want to admit

Janai. I shared with them how upset I was with her behavior from the moment she walked into the exam room, and how she did not care about the frightened young girl who was confused and crying in her mother's arms that afternoon. I went on and shared how she looked at me and her mind was already made up that we were not getting anymore of her time and she wanted us to leave. I told them that I knew I had to do everything I could do to get my child admitted, because this "white coat", did not hear or see me as a mother trying to save her precious child.

As I was sharing all of this information, that same "white coat" came walking down the hall towards us. She stopped right in front of Janai's room, looked at me, smiled, and said, "I understand that Janai had two seizures last night; I am the one who admitted her to this floor." I looked at her and said, "You are not to go into my daughter's room or speak to me about my daughter's condition, you are off Team Johnson and I will be reporting you to the medical director for your unprofessional behavior." I then turned around and finished my conversation with the surprised medical students, who did not know what to say, except "Who are you and what do you do?" I laughed and said, "I am Janai's mother, and that's all you need to know about me."

More lab results slowly came back, and all were still negative. Janai was beginning to get more agitated and nervous. Her speech was starting to become slurred, and she was very confused and could not even remember what happened the night before. I knew she had to be hungry and ordered her breakfast, but she did not eat anything. She just laid in her bed drifting further and further away from us.

What we knew so far was that there was an infection in Janai's brain, her white blood count was very high, and she had two seizures. The rest of that day involved more tests and talking to doctors, social workers, and meeting the nurses assigned to Janai's care. One particular group of health care professionals called "One to One" were assigned to our room. This group of caring professionals work with families that have children with various emotional, physical, and mental needs. Many suffer from brain injuries and autism. Our first assigned "One to One" was a beautiful young woman named Jessica. She was caring, funny, confident, and immediately connected with Janai and me. She was there to watch Janai and make sure she was safe and to help with her care along with the medical team. Jessica shared with me that she had worked with other young people with encephalitis, and we were at the right hospital for them to find the proper diagnosis and treatment. Many of the nurses had told me the same thing and I began to believe them all.

Janai was beginning to have several outbursts throughout the day and night that would warrant the nurses coming in to calm her, along with the "one to one." These outbursts were all part of her infection and I began to call them "Brain Inflamed Outburst" The goal was to identify the brain infection and treat it immediately. Janai had her third-seizure late Friday night and the nurses were there with me, we all became very concerned. The "white coats" increased her seizure medication and I requested the "Patient Information" (PI) on every drug that was given to Janai. I had my notebook along with my other folder, and started organizing all of her medical information.

The IV Team was sent to Janai's room, and to our surprise a beautiful and very friendly nurse showed up that Carvon and I both knew very well. Nurse T.B. was a member of our church and was very gentle with Janai. Later she told us that when she saw Janai's name, she never paid it much mind because she thought it was a coincidence, until she walked into our room and saw me sitting there. She prayed the entire time Janai was hospitalized and so did many others that we knew who worked at the hospital and they all became part of "Team Johnson's Medical Angels."

We had already spent two nights in the hospital, which really felt like a week. Janai was always healthy and had never spent the night in the hospital, except when she was born. Breakfast had arrived but she had no appetite because of her swollen tongue from the seizure. Janai still did not remember anything that had happened from earlier in the week. The nurses came around for their daily vitals and meds, and more tests were ordered.

Dr. Jona came in late that morning and sat down with me and went over every test result that came back and explained what they were and why they were performed. I took many notes and asked lots of questions, most of them he could answer. The one question he could not answer was "What is wrong with our daughter?" He was just as baffled as we were and many of the other specialists who were now coming from the University of Pennsylvania Hospital, which is located right across the street from Chop.

This was a Saturday, and we were still getting lots of visiting doctors. I was looking forward to seeing Jayla, and I knew she needed to see Janai and her Mommy. Damita and Wayne met Carvon at our house, and I gave Damita a list of things to bring with them to the hospital. Besides a few clothing items such as; three velour pants with matching jackets, toiletries, my Bible, my IPad, and a large binder, pens, and highlighters. I asked Damita to bring Janai's purple blanket, purple teddy bear that she had since she was five and a few of her favorite things from her bedroom. If we were going to be here for any length of time, I wanted Janai to feel as comfortable as I could possibly make her.

The meds the "white coats" had prescribed for Janai were altering her behavior dramatically. I had some concerns and expressed them. We weren't sure if it was the meds or the illness that was causing the behavior, either way, our daughter was not herself. Still, she seemed happy to see Jayla, Damita, and Wayne when they arrived. I could see the fear on their faces as they all looked at Janai and tried to be upbeat and hopeful. Jayla quietly sat next to me, and I saw the tears run down her face and at that moment, I knew she was scared for her big sister. God, how am I supposed to hold it all together once again.

The visit was not long because Janai became agitated and uncomfortable with everyone just sitting there, so Carvon took everyone to the hospital's family room to get themselves together and to pray. As soon as they all left, Janai cried and I knew she didn't want anyone to see her in that condition. Carvon and Jayla spent that night with us and I knew Janai was happy to have her family altogether, even if it was in a hospital room.

We all woke up that beautiful Sunday morning missing being at Christian Stronghold with our beloved Pastor Richardson and our church family. We knew that the whole congregation was praying for our daughter and we were so grateful and blessed. We all ate breakfast together and had our own church service in Janai's room. The soothing gospel music from the radio and Carvon reading scripture seemed to keep Janai calm. I had noticed too much stimulation agitated her and made her more nervous. We kept the room quiet and calm for the rest of that day. I took this opportunity to take Jayla to the cafeteria where we were able to talk. It was one of the most difficult conversations I had to have with my youngest daughter, who at the time was only twelve. I had to tell her that I would be staying in the hospital with Janai until she was better. Jayla cried and asked, "How long would that be?" it hurt me to tell her "I don't know baby." I told her I needed her to be a big girl and help Daddy and that all of her "Aunties" in our village would be there to help her. As a mother, what else could I have done or said.

I reminded her that I would stay and comfort Janai just like I did with her. We made a promise to call each other in the morning before she went to school, after school, and before she went to bed. I told my youngest daughter how much I loved her and that I was very proud of her for being Mommy's little big girl. Jayla cried and hugged me and then asked for a cell phone, only Jayla would see an opportunity and go for it. I told her I would consider it, given the circumstance.

We ate our lunch and continued to talk until Carvon called and said I needed to get back to the room. Janai had another outburst, and it was hard to calm her down, the nurses had to medicate her. I asked Carvon and Jayla to get ready to leave, and I was back in my caretaker's role. It seemed that I was the only one Janai would respond to. The rest of the night I prayed over my daughter and watched this illness slowly take my baby away from all of us.

Monday morning I woke up as I would if Janai and Jayla were getting ready for school, but instead, I was looking at my oldest daughter in a hospital bed. This particular morning was very hectic as many of the

"White Coats" were coming in to meet Janai, many of them were young med students from University of Penn. The new nurse and our "one to one" came in around 7:00am, and I immediately began speaking to them. I wanted to know how things operated in this hospital, especially on this floor. I started by asking for the schedules of the staff; the nurses, one to ones, attending physicians, fellows, and residents. I wanted to know with whom I would be interacting with regarding my daughter's care. We had been there for five days, and I still did not know who was our primary doctor in charge.

Carvon had brought two graduation pictures of Janai for us to have in her room. I wanted to show her this picture every day so she could see the beautiful and smart girl that lives within her. We put the other picture on her door for all who entered could see our beautiful Janai. I made sure they knew that what they saw lying in that bed was a child with an illness and that my daughter would come back to us. I also noticed Janai became very anxious when there were several people in the room and when she had to answer the same questions over and over. I came up with "Janai's Triggers and Tips" that I had typed up and put on her door along with her picture.

Janai's Triggers and Tips

1. Unfamiliar Faces
   -Janai benefits from consistency

2. Repetitive questions
   -Morning assessments by different people
   -Mom recommends one MD assess and discuss
    with other team members

3. People sitting near bedside
   -Janai recognizes this is not normal, and becomes afraid/agitated/confused.

4. Night Time
   -Janai is afraid of not waking up, therefore fights sleep
   -After 8 pm is Janai's hardest time
   -Noises bother her
   -Enjoys gospel music, keep music low
   -Keep dim lighting in room

5. Seeing Mom frustrated or angry with staff
   -Speak to mom outside of the room

6. Janai benefits from activity as redirection
   -Long walks down the hallways of the hospital
   -Exercising in her room

This list caused me many stares when the "White Coats" walked into our room. I was now sitting at the desk that I transformed into my hospital office space. When the "White Coates" entered, I had them sit in the chair near my makeshift desk. I was wearing my brown velour outfit with my matching leopard slippers and all my jewelry, especially my wedding ring. I knew what I was getting ready to face, I was a strong woman going up against dominant and sometimes arrogant men. Many times who you are is based on what is observed first. This was the case with some of the "White Coats" as they spoke to me and looked at how calm I was during one of the most difficult times of my life. This was now becoming my "normal behavior" so the MOM (Master of Many) came out, and I made sure I was always prepared, heard, seen and respected.

I started with my outfit, the "brown velour" and slippers. It became my hospital suit and I told the nurses if you see me with the "brown velour," you know I have a meeting in my office. The nurses laughed, but knew I was serious and I meant business. I was fighting for my child's life the best way I knew how. I could keep calm and keep my emotions in check when necessary, and only let my true emotions show to a very small group of friends and God.

Dr. Jona seemed to be my go to doctor, and he and I would have lengthy conversations about this unknown encephalitis. By now, I was doing my own research and calling on my own "Medical Team" of experts discussing every detail of Janai's care. Our "Medical Angels" were childhood and church friends as well as neighbors. Dr. Aliya, Dr. Heather, Dr. Pam, Dr. Stacey, Dr. Judy, Dr. Earl, Dr. Ross, Dawn, Wendy, Tonja and Lisa who were all respected professionals in the medical community. I was blessed to have each one of them on our team. They fed me medical information that I then relayed to the "White Coats;" it became funny when I would pull out my notepad and rattle off some medical questions for them to answer. Many of them would looked at me and wondered if I was a doctor, but all they needed to know about me was that I was Janai's mother.

Dr. Jona came later that day and looked very concerned as he asked to speak with me outside the room. I immediately began praying and then walked with him to a private area, took a seat near a window and braced myself for what he was about to say. He began to tell me about an autoimmune disease called anti-NMDA receptor encephalitis. He then explained what it is, how it was discovered and by whom, a neurologist from the University of Pennsylvania named Dr. Joseph Dalmau. "Anti-NMDA receptor encephalitis is a type of brain inflammation caused by antibodies, that are produced by the body's own immune system and that attack "NMDA" receptors in the brain. "NMDA" receptors are proteins that control electrical impulses in the brain."

Dr. Jona said he had suspected that this might be the rare illness Janai was experiencing and he encouraged me to learn all I could about it. By now my head was spinning, and I wanted to know what caused this condition in Janai. I was so confused and scared at the same time. Then, he and another doctor brought me a consent form to sign so that they could send away Janai's serum-fluid removed from her blood and CSF-cerebrospinal fluid from her spinal tap. This was all to be sent to Barcelona, Spain to be tested. Dr. Dalmau was there doing research on neurologic problems caused by a person's immune system. I needed to breathe and cry after receiving and hearing all of this critical medical information. I signed the consent form and then we waited for the results of my daughters's rare diagnosis.

Later that night I called Angel, Janai's Godmother, to inform her about Janai's medical condition. Angel was now living in Florida and I knew she would want to be with us. I had waited to call her because she was celebrating her 50th birthday with her family and parents who were visiting from Delaware, and I did not want to be the bearer of bad news. I stepped outside the room and found a little nook by the window. I looked outside and that evening sky was so beautiful, I took a minute just to get myself ready to speak to my best friend. Upon hearing my voice, Angel knew immediately that something was wrong. We spoke and cried that evening and I could hear the pain in her voice and she could hear mine. We prayed for Janai's healing, and I told her I would keep her updated as we found out more information. She told me to stay strong and to let her know if I needed her to come be with me. However, she knew I had a strong village surrounding us and praying for Janai and our family.

When Angel's Mom and Dad came home, they called me to see if I needed anything. I remembered speaking with them and wishing my mother was alive to be with me, as I was going through this medical nightmare. My only ask of them was to come and hug me. Within an hour, Adam and Jean who I affectionately call "Mom and Dad Harper" were walking down the hallway of the hospital to give me that hug I so needed. The nurses all saw the warm exchange when I walked out of Janai's room to meet them. In that brief moment, I let my body collapse and cried like a daughter in the loving arms of two people I needed the most. I still cry thinking of that day and the beautiful act of unconditional love.

We continued to monitor Janai's activity with daily medications and comprehensive neurological exams. Janai was asked to spell world backwards, count by seven to one hundred, count backwards from twenty, say the months of the year backwards, and draw a clock. All things she is more than capable of doing but had difficulties with all of them, due to her "inflamed brain." It was hard to sit and watch her struggle through these exams that I had memorized and could do in my sleep. We prayed and had many concerns, as Janai was not sleeping, becoming more agitated, experiencing loss of memory, and increasingly slurred speech. My daughter was disappearing into darkness right in front of me. The brain is a fascinating organ that remains a mystery to many.

We started off that next day with Dr. Jona informing us that Janai had developed an acute kidney injury, which the renal team believed was the result of the medications. So, we stopped one of the meds and waited for improvements. In the meantime, Janai was set up for an ultrasound of her ovaries to check for teratomas, (a type of germ cell tumor.) This horrible disease causes these tumors in female patients. As we waited for the results, the "White Coats" explained the procedure of removing the teratomas if any are present, and in rare cases removal of the ovaries. I wanted to cry right in front of them, but I held it together and prayed that no tumors would be found. I followed the team down to ultra sound and explained to Janai that they would have to take an X-ray of her ovaries and that Mommy would be right there with her. Janai looked at me for any signs of fear, and I showed her none. I have realized that my daughters look to me for strength, and I have shown them that Mommy gets her strength from God. I was trusting and believing God through this medical journey. Later that day the results came back negative, no teratomas were found and we counted this as a medical blessing.

Wow! One week at CHOP felt like a month! The "White Coats" were now hovering around our door looking over papers and discussing Janai's condition. Once again, I found myself waiting for information from them so I made a mental note to inform them that I wanted to be a part of their "daily grand rounds" regarding Janai.

I decided to use that time while I waited to speak to Jayla before she left for school. I was missing her and I hoped she knew how much I loved her. Carvon and the village of aunties were checking on her and making sure she had what she needed, it's been a very difficult for time for everyone. After speaking with my baby, I called her middle school and spoke to the counselor and school nurse to give them an update on our family's medical situation. I needed her school community to embrace her emotional needs and give her a safe place to share what and how she was feeling. It pays to have a good relationship with your school community, and I made sure we had that covered the day we entered The Council Rock School District. The high school counselor, nurse and teachers were all very concerned about Janai. It became very difficult for all of us to wrap our "brains" around the severity of her illness. I'm sure that knowing the illness was not contagious put everyone at ease.

I was juggling many things as most mothers do, but nothing was more important than getting Janai well. I had to keep a clear head and not allow fear to enter my mind. "To think clear there can be no fear." I wrote that along with many other pearls of wisdom in my journal. It was now 9:00am and I had accomplished all the things I needed to do regarding the girls' school.

The "White Coats" had just finished up discussing Janai's case and were now entering our room with more information to share. The medical team wanted to start Janai on a regimen of IV/IG, (immunoglobulin therapy) is therapy with antibody immunoglobulin mixtures, given intravenously and high doses of steroids to treat this form of encephalitis. I had read about and discussed the treatment with Carvon earlier in the week, and we both agreed that we would allow them to proceed with this course of therapy. Janai would receive the IV/IG as an infusion for five days and Methylprednisolone (Steroids) for four days, both beginning that day. For the first time all week, I felt that we were moving in the right direction, however we were still waiting for the results to come back from Barcelona, Spain. If Janai in fact had this rare form of encephalitis, the "White Coats" were being proactive and treating Janai aggressively with this combination of therapy.

My daughter was very sick and every second of the day I watched her drifting further away. I continued with my prayers, and I would not be human if I was not asking God "why," but I knew the "who" and knowing that God was with me, brought me comfort and peace.

The nurses entered the room and set Janai up for her first round of treatment, as I watched and took notes on how it was administered. I also asked for the (PI) on the two new drugs to add to my files. She was very calm, and I reassured her that this treatment was going to make her well. She looked at me and said nothing, but I could tell by her eyes that she was trusting me. I told Janai every day that I loved her and that Mommy was not going anywhere. When she opened her eyes in the morning, I was the first person she saw and the last person when she fell asleep. Many nights she had me sleep in the bed with her, and I did just what she requested, a Mother's Love for Janai.

Once again I found myself waiting and watching for any signs. The one to ones are with us around the clock and I have found them all to be very comforting for Janai and me too. Janai was getting very familiar with them all, and they seemed to work well with her. It was very strange to have someone you don't know in the room with you at your bedside all the time, even when you sleep, just watching you.

Janai tolerated the new therapy well and we were getting ready for day two of treatment. It was a Friday morning, and I had not left the room since we were admitted 10 days ago. I walked down to the cafeteria to get a bagel and hot tea. I then walked outside to breathe in this cold and crisp January air. It was a little thing, but it made me feel energized and I needed that to continue on this journey. I came back to the fifth-floor, and Janai had been looking for me. I had picked up a bagel for her as well, but she was still not eating or drinking which was a concern for the medical staff. I had suggested they give her vanilla milkshakes mid day with the hope she would drink something I knew she enjoyed.

Janai was resting after her second-treatment, and I was writing in my journal the day the doctors received the results from Dr. Dalmau in Spain. As they suspected, it was now confirmed that my daughter has anti-NMDA receptor encephalitis. Janai was now part of a medical case study and the documentation was now beginning. I was relieved we finally had a positive diagnosis and the right treatment plan in action, but all I wanted was my daughter back.

We were all hoping her body would begin to heal from this treatment. I called to let the village know and I could hear the questions coming, but I answered none of them. The shock of hearing that your daughter has been diagnose with a rare brain infection is very hard to comprehend. I was praying that it would not be this illness as I began to do my own research, it's an ugly disease. I was heart broken, and then I remembered God's promise, "she will be healed for all to see." I just didn't know when, but I trusted God's word to me.

It was the morning of day three of Janai's treatments of the IV/IG and steroids. Janai had not slept well and seemed more agitated. The medical team and I decided to adjust her medication, in hopes that she would be able to sleep. Janai was more tired after her treatments and seemed so lifeless just lying in that bed. I played music for her and continued to speak to my daughter even in her silence. Throughout the day, Janai continued to have outbursts that required medical attention, most of the time I was the one keeping her calm. Her "brain is inflamed" and she does things and says things that she cannot control. Her words were are all jumbled together and it became very difficult to understand her. She also could not write in her tablet which frustrated her even more. Her beautiful smile and her eloquent speech have been replaced by silence and lack of facial expression. It was as if she had already died inside.

My sister Tina had arrived early that evening with dinner and all of Janai's favorite things to eat. To our surprise, she did try to eat a little something, especially her favorite peach cobbler. It was very hard for my sister to see Janai in this state but she held it together, like I knew she would. This was not the time or place to lose it, and I gave my sister that look that only she understood. Tina brought me more items to transform Janai's hospital room into something more comforting and more like home. We decorated the room and even the bathroom that night. Janai had not spoken at all to Tina while she was visiting until she said "Aunt Tina you have to go now." I looked at Tina and saw Janai was getting very agitated. I kissed Tina and said goodnight, and thanks to Janai, Tina made it home safely before the unexpected snow storm. Tina was one of the few people that I allowed to visit us in the hospital.

Just when I thought things could not get any worse, later that night Janai had two major seizures and was transferred immediately to ICU (Intensive Care Unit) on the seventh-floor. We arrived to the ICU and were met by a new team of "white coats." The attending physician on call that evening, whom I immediately connected with, was a tremendous help to me. Janai stayed in the ICU for three-days, and had two more seizures while there. She was hooked up to so many monitors and had so many nurses coming in the room as I sat next to her bed praying over her.

Her seizures now a total of 7 were now a major concern for the medical team, and we had to get them under control quickly. She was put on Topamax and was being watched very carefully. Once stable, she was transferred from ICU to Neurology on the ninth-floor. We settled in our new room and Janai continued to slip deeper and deeper away from us all. By now "The White Coats" were hoping to see some improvements from the five days of the IV/IG therapy and the high dosage of steroids. To me, Janai was getting worse and so were the seizures. I met new "White Coates" from Neurology as they changed so frequently throughout this hospital.

All of my "White Coats" from the fifth-floor, I no longer saw. In this case, I believed that one doctor should have been our primary go to "White Coat" throughout Janai's care. Nevertheless, I made our "Team Johnson" work the best way I knew how. Janai was to remain on this floor for the duration of her stay, so I requested a specific "White Coat" that could answer questions I might have about my daughter's illness.

The nurses on the floor had not had many patients with this type of rare autoimmune, and were not familiar about the many aspects of this type of illness. I had to educate them all, and the last time I checked, I had not gone to any medical school, but felt as though I had received many medical degrees while on this journey. I asked to meet with the nurse managers so I could brief them on Janai's condition and triggers, hoping that they would then educate their entire staff. I really thought we would be back on the fifth-floor where they knew us, instead we were starting all over again with a new team of "White Coats" and nurses. The rest of that week went very slowly as Janai was getting familiar to the new team of "White Coats." Janai was also getting adjusted to new medications and her therapies throughout the day, as I was putting out fires everywhere.

I had a visit from a social worker speaking to me about Janai's continued medical care, once she was discharged from Chop. She shared with me our options of rehabilitation facilities for children who suffer from brain injuries. CHOP does have one, but Janai was not guaranteed a private room. I began my own research on facilities in our area and decided on Moss Rehab in Elkins Park, Pa. The social worker began the process and told me she would get back with me once she got confirmation on availability.

One of Janai's triggers was consistency, which she did not have moving to the ninth-floor. This caused my daughter to become irritable and that made me become aggravated. The "one to ones" that she was comfortable with, were no longer available to her, and the nurse managing staff was putting nursing students in our room. A nursing student was not equipped to handle Janai and her "Brain Inflamed Outbursts." I witnessed several of the nursing students panic when Janai had an outburst. I asked what are you to do and what training have you received; all replied none, my point exactly! I then asked for the nurse manager who is responsible for putting together the schedules of the "one to ones." I was so surprised how quickly the nurses gave me her name and chuckled as they left my room and asked me about the "brown suit?" I see the word traveled from floor to floor about me and my brown business attire. After several messages, I finally met with her, shared my dilemma, and requested that Janai have consistency with her trained and experienced "one to ones." She informed me of the process of selecting them for the patients and did not take my request seriously. I paused for a moment and thought of how I was going to get my message across to this woman who obviously did not understand my request and urgency. I looked at her, as

99

she was quite nervous speaking with me as I pulled out the hospital's Mission Statement, which I had in my large binder highlighted along with the names of the executive team. I then asked her what the qualifications were for the "ones to ones" and their responsibilities to the patients and the responsibilities for the "nursing students" here at this hospital. We continued this back and forth conversation until she agreed with me that they made a mistake by putting a student with no training in the room with Janai. The idea of me being with Janai was to watch over my daughter and make sure that she was given the best treatment and care by the medical team at CHOP.

The nursing staff became used to seeing me every day and night. They were briefed about me before entering Janai's room. I knew all the medications they would be bringing to her and always asked to see the meds before she took anything. On one occasion while changing shifts, a nurse brought in her meds that she was just given. I was sitting in my chair reading and the nurse came in to let me know that she would be on duty that evening and had Janai's medication. I asked her, "did you debrief with the nurse who just left?" She had not, nor had she read Janai's chart. Very politely I asked her to go and read the previous notes. She then asked, "Are you writing everything down?" I kindly replied "Everything." She later apologized, and I smiled and told her to always read the notes and that if a parent or caregiver is in the room, speak with them about the care of their loved one. I had this conversation with all the nurses that cared for Janai during our stay, we were very fond of them all.

The social worker came back in to see me and to tell me the good news, Moss had availability and Janai would be leaving CHOP. Janai heard her and thought she was going home. I pulled the social worker outside and told her that Janai is not medically stable enough to be discharged and asked to whom she had spoken too. She had not spoken to any of the "White Coats" and spoke prematurely. This misunderstanding should have never happened and once again, there was no consistency in the communication amongst the medical staff. I had to calm Janai down and tell her that we were not leaving Chop that day, but soon.

Twenty-days we have spent at Children's Hospital and Janai was not getting any better. She continued with her daily physical, occupational and speech therapies with great difficulty. Her communication, orientation and some emotional behaviors and responses were all impaired. It was very hard for me to see Janai struggle with recalling greater than two words in a word series recall task. She had difficulty recalling what she had eaten for breakfast yesterday or lunch one hour prior to eating. Janai knew who I was and would say to me often "Mommy, please don't leave me," It was always in a soft voice and very childlike.

I would work with Janai once the therapists left and my sessions were productive. Her brain continued to be inflamed, and she had many outbursts during the day that warranted sedation, but I intervened and kept her calm without any sedatives. I believed that the brain had to heal on its own. The "White Coats" would watch from the door and were amazed at how calm she became with my techniques, which were to firmly hold and rock her, speak softly, look directly in her eyes and tell her that I loved her and that God loved her more. I repeated this technique as often as she needed, which happened to be two or three times a day.

February 14, we all celebrated our Valentine's Day in the hospital. My dear friend Alisa had brought decorations and sweet treats for us to celebrate and share with the medical staff. I had decorated Janai's room with red hearts, balloons, and a tablecloth with matching napkins. All who entered received a card, chocolate covered strawberries, and an assortment of chocolates. Janai seemed calm and I even saw her smile when the "White Coats" came to give her a special Valentines card. The nurses all told me that they never saw the "White Coats" give any patient a card that had been signed by the entire team. I told them they never met anyone like "Team Johnson." They all laughed and said, "No, they never met anyone like Robyn Johnson." I must admit, I had shaken up this hospital, in a positive way of course.

Later that same day and one of my bold moves was to call up to the executive floor and speak with Steven Altschuler, the Chief Executive Officer at the time. I called and his secretary informed me that Mr. Altschuler was out of the country and she could take a message for me. It was really funny because she could tell I was calling from the hospital, and that piqued her curiosity. I shared with her that I was indeed in the hospital with my daughter and we had been there almost a month. I wanted to speak and share with the CEO, Mr. Altschuler all of my observations and concerns. I thought he would enjoy meeting and speaking with me. Since he was not in, I asked to speak with Madeline Bell, president and COO. I left a message for her several times while I was at Chop.

Eventually, someone from the "Executive Suite" came to meet with me. I shared with her that for the most part I was very pleased with the care that my daughter was receiving, however there were several incidents that needed to be addressed.

My concerns were the following:

1. No consistent sharing of medical information with the other departments among the "White Coats." I would often have to bring other "White Coats" up to date with information that they should have been aware of.

2. Because of my daughter's condition, we would see Neurology, Psychiatry, Adolescent Medicine, Nephrology, Oncology, Infectious Disease and other "White Coats" from CHOP and University of Pennsylvania. Some of them lacked professionalism and courtesy with Janai, with me and even with one another.

3. I had to contact the medical director and file a formal complaint on two "White Coats," both females. The one who would not admit Janai in the ER and another "White Coat" who came to our room with a resident to examine Janai. I had to bring her up to speed on Janai's condition. They really don't read the charts before walking into a patient's room. I had questions to ask the doctor, who looked at me and said, I don't have time to answer your questions, I have other patients to see. I looked at her and asked, When you are finished, may you come back and speak with me, I have concerns about the medication and my daughter's lack of sleep. I need to speak with a "White Coat" and you are the Attending physician this week on this floor. She was rude and told her "Resident" to handle my questions. Later that evening, the resident came in to apologize about her superior's lack of professionalism. I told her to never apologize for someone else's bad behavior and I called the medical director on her immediately.

I knew they were ready for "Team Johnson" to be discharged from this hospital, and never seen again. The hospital executive spoke with me for a while as she wrote down all of my concerns, four-pages. I had closed the door and the nurses knew that Janai was in therapy, but that did not stop them from wondering who was in the room. They never knew who was coming to see me at any given time of the day or night. I liked keeping them all guessing.

On Sunday, February 17, Damita and Sydney were coming to visit Janai, and this would be Sydney's first time seeing Janai since she was admitted. The girls were like sisters and had been together since birth. I knew the visit would be emotional for both of them. Damita and I were prepared as only mothers could be. Sydney was very nervous when she saw Janai, and began to cry. Janai called out to her "sissy," as she affectionately calls her, and gave her a big hug. The two of them stayed that way for a long time in front of the nurse's station. I saw the tears from Janai's nurses, and I was touched. Janai had often spoken about Sydney to them, and now they finally got a chance to witness this special sisterly bond of friendship and love.

Damita had brought us a beautiful lunch, and we all sat in the family area and ate. It was a nice afternoon, and Janai seemed to have enjoyed seeing her best friend. I was hoping this visit would be just what she needed and that she finally would be able to have a good night's sleep. Instead, she cried with pain all night. Janai missed her life, and it pained me to see her so sad. That night as I held her in my arms, as I had done many times before, I cried the sadness and pain with her.

On Monday, we got a visit from Dr. Ryan, the "White Coat" who worked with Dr. Dalmau and who was familiar with anti-NMDA Receptor Encephalitis. She examined

Janai along with Dr. Williams, who also is a neurologist. I asked why it took her so long to visit my daughter. We had been there twenty-six days and we're now seeing her, "the expert," for the first time. I let her know this delay was unacceptable. She looked at me as many of the others had done and responded by saying "she was kept informed of Janai's case." I then replied to her, "You have the most experience with this illness and many of my questions and concerns could have been answered by YOU!, and not by other "White Coats" who were not familiar with this horrible illness."

I had lots of questions for her and she did answer them, but they were not much more than I had already known or found out on my own. This condition was still considered a "rare autoimmune disease," and there wasn't much medical literature published. After our meeting and exam, they both agreed that Janai was medically stable to move to the rehabilitation phase of this medical journey.

Later that night, I was so exhausted from all the earlier meetings and on the phone with my sister, I shared that I was hungry and craving a taste for seafood. She said to call "Bottom of the Sea." My cousin "Porky," whose real name is "Gregory," had worked there. I called and surprisingly he answered the phone, I hadn't spoken to him in many years. I shared that I had been in the hospital almost a month with my daughter and just wanted something different to eat. He was so concerned and told me that I could have anything I wanted, and he would have it delivered to the hospital. I thanked God that I got the chance to talk with him when I did, a brief call that I would cherish forever.

We soon readied ourselves for the transfer to Moss Rehabilitation. The nurses and "White Coats" all came in to say goodbye and to help us pack. Many had given me personal notes, wishing us the best and wanting to keep in touch. I knew that we would have to come back for treatments, but that would be in a different building. I had all the medications that Janai was on and the times she would get them once we arrived. I was getting all of my medical records and notes together as I did not know what to expect once we got there. I had so many questions going through my mind and was somewhat nervous, because we had to start all over again. I was ready, but were they ready for "Team Johnson?"

We had spent twenty-eight days in Children's Hospital, and I had slept every night next to my daughter on a sofa bed. I never left that hospital until we were being transferred to Moss Rehabilitation in Elkins Park, Pa., Let the Medical Journey continue...

Moss Rehabilitation

*The healing of mind, body and soul
is the source of joy.*

It was a Wednesday evening, and we were being transferred by ambulance to begin our next phase of Janai's medical journey. It was very familiar to me because it was the old Rolling Hill Hospital in Elkins Park, and I used to have this territory when I worked as a senior pharmaceutical sales representative. We met in the waiting area until someone from the Brain Injury Unit came to escort Janai to her room. I knew Janai was scared and did not want to be there. We all got into the elevator and went to the fourth-floor. Janai was in a wheelchair and I was holding her hand as we went through the multiple doors. We had to be buzzed in and then wait for the doors to close behind us and then buzzed in again to enter the patient floor.

We finally got to room 488, which was small with a bed, a chair, and a closet. There was a window and a sink off to the left of the bed and a bathroom with no shower or bath tub. This room was going to be our home for as long as it took to get Janai healed. We settled in and I quickly spoke with the doctor and nurse on duty that evening. We did what we could that night, but I knew the morning would be a different situation. I tried to get Janai to sleep that night, but the noises coming from the hallway kept us both awake. This was a floor of patients that had suffered traumatic brain injuries (TBI). Janai did not really fall under this category, but I felt that the rehabilitation therapies would be of great benefit to her. I had done my research on this facility and more importantly, I wanted to stay with her.

At 7:00am the nurse walked in to get Janai's vitals and her medication. She was still taking the anti-seizure medication and others to help with her agitation. I kept up with them all and continued to write in my journal what was given to my daughter. This facility was not like CHOP and had a lot of activity going on all day long. The patients' doors all remained open so you could see them as you walked by each room. Our room was across from the laundry room and near the nurses station. I was told that we would have a meeting at 8:00am with Janai's team of therapists and the nursing staff. I got dressed with my brown velour suit and slippers, I was ready!

I put Janai's triggers on the door along with her graduation picture, as I had done at CHOP. I started to decorate her room and get us settled in as I was told we would be there for at least six-eight weeks. They gave me a reclining chair to sleep in as I told them I would be staying with my daughter, the entire time. Once again they had no idea about "Team Johnson." I had my notes and all of her medical records with me. I was prepared for this meeting, but they were not prepared for me. Janai and I were introduced to her three therapists; Physical Therapy (PT) was Meagan, Occupational Therapy (OT) was Allison, and Speech Therapy (SLP) was Deb. Dr. Marino and Dr. Connors were also in this meeting who we already met last night when we arrived. The nurse manager was Lisa and the clinical manager was Nicole. It was our own grand rounds, I gave them the history of Janai and brought them up to speed. Once again, they had never treated a patient with this exact illness. We went over her medications and her schedule and what a typical day of therapy would look like for her. This was going to be a challenge for Janai, because she was not sleeping.

Our first day of therapy was not successful and could not be completed because she was very agitated and confused. The medication along with being extremely tired caused her to have difficulties focusing on simple tasks. She wanted to leave several times and go back to her room and lay down. When she could not, she became agitated and very upset. We discussed adding another medication to help her to focus. I told them it was going to be difficult for her to adjust to her new surroundings and to give her some time. I was there to help them understand my daughter and this illness. That weekend was also very difficult because I was not given her schedule before our nurse left. Janai needed consistency, and so did I.

The "White Coat" on duty for the weekend walked into our room without reading the chart and looked at Janai lying in bed and asked if she had been in a car accident. I looked at her as Janai became very excited and said "Mommy was I in an accident" and she then began to cry. I quickly said "no sweetheart you were not in an accident and you are going to be fine." I then asked to speak with the "White Coat" outside the room. I told her to never come into a room without reading a patient's chart, take that extra minute or two and read the highlights. She apologized to me and agreed to do just that. I then began to tell her about my daughter and showed her the picture on the door. She then re-entered the room with a totally different approach. Janai did not have any PT scheduled that first weekend; however, PT was scheduled that Saturday, but I was not notified at all. The nurse never informed me of her schedule even after I had inquired before they left for the weekend.

Janai's therapies for Saturday
9:00-9:30 am- Speech Therapy
2:00-2:30 pm- Occupational Therapy
3:00-3:30 pm- Physical Therapy

She went to all of her scheduled therapies and rested as she complained of lower back pain. The doctor did give her medication and it seemed to ease some of her pain. The rest of the weekend I would take her for a walk to the cafeteria and the gift shop and then we would get back on the elevator back to her room. It was very boring there on the weekends and if she was not active she would just sleep. I tried everything to keep her up so she could sleep at night. Janai's schedule was off, and it was like having a newborn all over again. However, I could not sleep while she slept at different times of the day.

Carvon and Jayla came to visit Janai over the weekend, and it was nice to have the family together. They always brought food from the many families that were preparing meals for Carvon and Jayla. They would bring Janai beautiful cards and gifts from all of her friends from church and school, who all missed her so much. Two of her best friends, James and Desi whom all met in elementary school, were devastated and missed their "sister" the most. They wanted to see her and felt so helpless. I knew that they cared for her and were praying that she would come home soon. I put up all of her cards and gifts all around her room so she could see how much she was loved. I would read to her every card and note when she received them. The nurses even would come in the room and read all the names on her board. I do believe my daughter felt the love and prayers from our village of supporters.

The visits with the family always made me feel stronger. However, my youngest daughter Jayla needed me more than I knew. She cried and begged me to come home just for a day. This was the longest I had been away from her and she was missing her mother and I was missing her too. I told her that I would start coming home on the weekends in March. That Sunday night after Carvon and Jayla left, Janai had a really bad night. She cried all night, and I stayed up with her the entire time. The visits were starting to affect her, she wanted to go home.

Monday mornings were always busy, and I had my notes from the weekend to go over with the nurses and the doctors. My concerns were:

1. Therapy schedules were not communicated to Mom for the weekend.

2. The on call doctor did not read the patient's chart before entering the room and assumed the patient was in a car accident.

3. One of the medications I would like to stop because of the side effects I saw over the weekend. It was making her more confused.

4. I would be going home on the weekends and returning on Monday mornings. My husband would be coming to be with Janai.

It was a productive meeting, and they were in agreement with me about stopping the medication. However, they were nervous about me leaving Janai over the weekend. Janai responded to me more than she did with anyone else. Janai began eating better and her sleeping through the night started to become more normal. She had not had any seizures since we left CHOP, and I prayed that she would remain seizure free.

I had soon made friends with the other parents on the floor and started a prayer group. While our children were in therapy, we would meet by the elevators on the floor and pray and talk about the care of our children. I heard many heartbreaking stories, and I prayed with each one of them. I became the Mother Advocate, and many of them called upon me to act on their behalf with the staff. They all said, "The staff responds to you and your requests." We became a family of caregivers on the fourth-floor. I would walk down the halls and speak to each family and give words of encouragement. I had to keep myself busy as well. If I wasn't writing in my journal the day to day of my daughter's care, I was helping out with the care of others on our floor.

It was a Thursday afternoon and Janai was in therapy. I was sitting in her room alone, waiting for her to come back, when my cell phone rang. When I saw that it was my sister, I knew something was wrong. My family and friends knew not to call me during the day, unless I sent a message that I was free to talk. I picked up the phone, and she was crying hysterically. She said she received a message that our cousin "Porky," whom we had spoken with, just two weeks prior, had been killed! My cousin who had delivered the seafood to me at CHOP, she told me it was all over the news. I said to her, "get yourself together, so you can drive home safely." I then stayed on the phone with her until she arrived home.

Afterwards, I turned on the news and saw my cousin's face, and the caption stated that the police were looking for a close family member. I then called Carvon to make him aware of this horrific news before he heard or saw it on tv. I had a strong feeling who that family member might be, and I was praying I was wrong.

Later that day, the breaking news gave the name of the family member, and it was my brother. My brother was being accused of taking the life of a love one, as I sat here fighting to save the life of a love one. The irony of this was overwhelming. I turned off the television as Janai was coming back to the room. She looked at me and said "Mommy, what is wrong?" and I responded "nothing sweetheart, Mommy is ok." I could hear my phone ringing, but I silenced it. I sat in my chair crying inside while I knew my family was being torn apart. I was in shock and wanted to call my Aunt to give my condolences, but something told me to sit still and pray.

My cousin "Porky" was a great man, son, brother, father, uncle, and friend to everyone who met him. He was a community activist and mentored many youth in the neighborhood. My heart was breaking, and I could not do anything to stop this pain. I replayed our last conversation over in my head and smiled when he told me that day was his day off. I knew God intended for me to call exactly when I did. I still can't believe he is gone. The kindness that he had shown me just two weeks prior would be how I remember him forever.

That evening Carvon and Jayla came to visit, and I needed to see them both. I was trying so hard to be strong, but this was difficult. That night I could not sleep and I cried out to God for help. This was too much, and I felt my chest tightening and my whole body ached. I wanted this pain, all of it, to stop. As I laid in the chair; balled up like a baby, I felt God's presence and comfort. I knew I could not save my brother this time and my heart ached for him. All I could do was pray for his soul and give it all to God, and that night, I released it all.

I looked at my daughter lying in her bed, and I knew that I had to find that inner strength to continue to be strong for Janai, who was fighting her way back. That morning I awoke with a sense of purpose and fighting spirit to continue this "Journey back to Joy."

For the first time since Janai was hospitalized, I was going home to spend the weekends with my youngest daughter Jayla. I was concerned about her, and I needed to spend time with her alone. I knew that once Janai was moved to Moss and we had a schedule that I was comfortable with, I could leave her with Carvon for the weekends.

Jayla needed her mother, and I knew that I had been blessed to be able to stay with Janai every day and be her caretaker. I had talked to Janai about my leaving, and she was very nervous and kept asking me if I was coming back. I told her my schedule and assured her that Mommy would never leave her and I would be back on Monday mornings after I dropped Jayla off at school. The rest of that day I could see that Janai did not want me to leave her, and she became frightened. I was torn between leaving my child without me, to go home to a child I left without me. Both my daughters needed my love and I was trying my best to do it all.

Forty-one days had passed since I had been home with Jayla, and I was looking forward to a hot bath and a good night's rest in my own bed. When Carvon arrived and it was time for me to leave Janai, tears began falling from her face. I looked at my daughter and told her that she was strong and getting stronger every day. I told her that God is with her and how much I loved her. I needed her to understand that Jayla needed me too. I kissed and hugged her tightly and left the hospital.

For the first time in forty-one days, I was alone without any "White Coats," hospitals, nurses, "one to ones," it was just me. On the way home I cried like I had never cried before. I was able to get it all out of my body, which I held in for forty-one days. It felt so good to release all that pain. I drove up my driveway and entered my garage, I was finally home. I walked into the house and Jayla ran towards me and gave me the biggest hug and held on to me and would not let me go. I stood in my kitchen and took it all in, closing my eyes and remembering that day in January when Janai came home from school crying. A scared girl that new something was not right and all she wanted was her joy back. Jayla was still holding on to me and I had to pry her fingers from my waist, I knew she was happy to see me and have me home, even if it was just a weekend.

My house looked and smelled just the way I had left it. Carvon knew I was very particular about our home and liked it to be kept clean and organized. However, this time I really could have cared less what the house looked like. I was happy to be home, even if it was only for a moment. Carvon had left dinner in the refrigerator that our village was still bringing to him and Jayla. He left me a piece of apple pie made with love from our dear sister friend Aliya. I finally settled in, got a glass of wine, and exhaled for the very first time.

After dinner, I took my long hot bubble bath, lit candles in my bathroom, and finished my glass or two of wine. I was relaxed for the first time in a long while. I put on my pajamas to get ready for my "heart to heart" with Jayla. My baby girl generally kept everything inside and would not share her feelings with anyone but me. Even after Carvon's battle with depression, and we were all in therapy, Jayla was still not comfortable sharing our family's problems. She would always say she was ok, and as her mother, I knew better. We both snuggled into my bed, and once she was settled, she began to cry and tell me how difficult this has been for her. Jayla was in pain and scared for her sister. Our family was in another crisis and Jayla, who would be thirteen later that year, and had been through so much of her own medical crisis, knew this feeling oh so well.

We spoke for hours that night, talking and crying. I knew that she was trying to be strong and keep it all together, as she has seen me do many times. I reminded her that I had to help Janai get through this journey, just like I was there for her, when she had her eye injury and many surgeries. I told her that we all have to be there for Janai and help her through. I also let her know that I would start coming home on the weekends to spend time with her, and that made her very happy. We both eventually fell asleep, her sleeping peacefully, wrapped in my arms.

That morning I called Janai as promised and we spoke for a long time as she kept asking me when I was coming back. I told her again that I would be there on Monday. She repeated the same question every time I spoke to her over that first weekend. Carvon said all was well, and I was pleased with that report. That Saturday morning Jayla and I went out for breakfast, shopping and got manicures. It was like our normal routine with the girls on the weekends. I knew that this was just what Jayla needed, because she did not open up about her sister to anyone at school. I was in contact with her counselor and asked that she check in with Jayla regularly to make sure she was ok. I also made all of her teachers aware of our family crisis and they were very accommodating to her needs as I requested.

Jayla was still under a doctor's care and was seen every second Tuesday of every month. I had to coordinate her schedule with friends if Carvon was not available to take her. Dr. Park would call me after Jayla's appointments and give me an updated report.

I tried to do as much as I humanly could do with Jayla that first weekend home. I knew that Monday mornings would be very difficult to leave her. We began a routine of having breakfast together and talking before I dropped her off to school. I knew she would cry, but she also knew that I would be coming home on Fridays. I was now known as "The Weekend Mommy."

I also took the time on Monday's to go into the girl's school to speak personally with their counselor and nurse. I wanted them all to be updated with Janai's condition as well as talk about Jayla. These were productive meetings and many questions were asked and answered face to face. Everyone was now briefed and my job was done.

I would get back to Moss mid-morning and I knew Janai would be in therapy. Carvon and I would have a chance to talk alone before she returned back to her room. The last couple of years had really taken a toll on our marriage and fixing it would take more than a conversation over a hot cup of tea. I had to leave all of that up to God, because my priority at that moment was our daughters. We talked about his first weekend with Janai, and I could tell he was ready to leave. Carvon was still battling with his own depression and stress; and was very uncomfortable being there with his daughter, as she was battling with the unknown.

It was hard for him to see his oldest child suffering like she was, and any parent would feel that way. Carvon had seen both his daughters suffer, but sadly, he could not relieve their suffering or pain. We prayed

117

together, I kissed him on his cheek and off he went back home to be with Jayla for the rest of the week until the next weekend.

Janai was so happy to see me. She gave me the biggest hug and said, "Mommy you came back," and I said to her, "Of course Mommy was coming back." The entire staff seemed very happy to see me as well. I got right back into my groove and started setting up her appointments for that week. Our first appointment was on Tuesday, March 5, at Chop. We had to make sure we had a "one to one" with us, as well as a nurse, and transportation. I requested the "one to one" I wanted and the nurse who would accompany us to the hospital for her continued immunotherapy treatments.

That evening I told Janai that we would be going to Chop for an appointment as part of her healing. I needed her to be aware of what was happening and to be comfortable and not be surprised. I was not sure how she would feel going back to CHOP, and I was not taking any chances on missing that appointment. I prayed that evening that all would go well in the morning and I didn't sleep much that night. When I looked at the clock, it was already 6:00am and I was ready. I had already prepared the staff for that day, so they knew the agenda.

Janai was not scheduled for any therapies that day because I did not want her to be agitated or too tired for the trip to CHOP. I was dressed and ready for the nurse when she came in to take Janai's vitals and to ask if I needed anything. I think she was very nervous because she and the rest of the staff had never had a patient like Janai or a mother like me. Also, I was not sure if the staff knew Janai was being transported to CHOP. As they checked and double-checked everything, I let Janai rest until it was time for our pick-up.

Once we arrived, I checked Janai into the Outpatient Oncology Department. I sat down and held Janai's hand as I watched the many children come in and out of the room where they were getting their chemo treatments. Many were so young and I could see the pain on the faces of the mothers or caregivers who were with them. I sat and prayed for their strength as well as my own as we waited to meet with Drs. Williams and Ryan who saw Janai when she was a patient in the hospital.

They called our names and I sat in the room while they examined my child and answered all of their questions, I had many concerns and I spoke about them as well. They agreed that Janai's progress was slow and she needed more treatments. The Immunotherapy Plan of action was put in place that day, and she would be seen every week for one month and then reevaluated. Janai would have her treatments in the Alex Scott Day Hospital, which provides outpatient oncology services and hematology transfusion services.

The treatment plan was; IV/IG, Dexamethasone and Rituximab which was something new they added. Once again, I had to sign a consent form for this treatment. Janai was on this combination in the hospital, and I made sure that it was to continue while she was at Moss. As a parent, you must do your homework and research everything. Moss did not administer this kind of treatment plan, and I knew she would have to be transported back and forth to CHOP for follow up visits. I asked how we would do this before I had Janai transferred to Moss Rehab. This was a new request for Moss as well.

Once the examination was over and all the questions and concerns were addressed, we now had a plan that we all agreed on. We also agreed that Janai had not progressed back to her baseline and that more tests were to follow her treatments. I shared that she had not had any seizures and continued with the anti seizure medication. She had developed improved insight into her present condition and knew that something about her was different. I continued to pray that my baby would get her joy back. Dr. Williams ordered a repeat LP and blood drawn for anti-NMDA receptor titers. He also scheduled a repeat MRI for tumors of the ovaries. He was hoping to see more improvement from Janai after she was discharged from the hospital.

This autoimmune is different in each patient, and you must treat the patient according to their symptoms. I was hopeful that the second round of treatments would be what Janai needed. Before leaving, I confirmed the next four-weeks of her appointments. Overall, it was a productive and enlighten day. We returned later that afternoon, and I had a meeting with Dr. Marino, the rehabilitation physician and Lisa, the nurse manager. I updated them on Janai's Plan of Action. I had taken copious notes, so good they wanted a copy. I told them they would be getting the doctors' notes faxed over to them the next day.

The rest of that week I noticed changes in Janai's appetite and questioned one of the medications. I was making my own notes and asked for a meeting to discuss my concerns and the dosage. In the middle of all of this, I always found time to meet and help other families that were staying on the fourth-floor. While Janai would be in her therapy session, I would sit in her room reading my bible with the door open. This particular day a man knocked on the door and asked if I would pray with him, I said "absolutely." His name was John and his son had been between University of Penn and Moss for a year. His son had a bad fall and hit his head the previous summer, John and his wife were told he was not going to make it. I then prayed over his son as well. John asked me if I could look out for his wife Lisa, who would need a friend when he had to travel back and forth home, which was out of the country. Once again, I said yes. I met with Lisa and she knew right away who I was and we began praying regularly. We would often have conversations about our children and the lives we hoped they would have. It was comforting to have those "heart to heart" conversations with the parents I had met on the fourth-floor, they were all very special to me, then and now.

I was going home for the second weekend to be with Jayla, and I really needed to get away. I cried again as I left Janai, telling her that I would be back on Monday. I got home early this time and did my routine, getting a bath and exhaling and Jayla and I had our Friday night "heart to heart" updates. On Saturday, March 9, Jayla celebrated my twenty-second wedding anniversary by going out to dinner and shopping with me. We had a beautiful evening and I tried to make the best of it. That Sunday afternoon, I made as many calls as I could, but I was overwhelmed and emotionally tired. I didn't realize how much had happened since January, and we still had a long way to go.

The weekend was over and I drove Jayla to school that Monday morning, kissed my baby, and told her we would talk later that afternoon. I had a lot to do, so I kept it moving once I got back to the fourth-floor. I scheduled the reservation for the transport for Janai's first treatment at the Wood Building of CHOP, where she was scheduled for a spinal tap and blood work in the morning and her Immunotherapy treatment in the afternoon. I also had to make arrangements for Jayla's appointment with Dr. Park and called on my sister friend Carla. I had to call on my village to help because

Carvon would be meeting us at the hospital for her first treatment. Everything was scheduled for the next day and I prayed that all would go well. It was going to be a long day for my daughter and I was concerned. She was anxious and I had to keep her calm. I had to think of a strategy, but that seemed to be very difficult because she was also having bad menstrual cramps. Yes, her cycle was coming on and I had to manage that as well. I was smart to bring the sanitary pads with me when I went home, because I was told there were no pads on the floor for the patients. They would have to order them as a special request. I then asked that they give her something for her pain that evening so she could sleep. Of all the nights, Janai was up tossing and turning in pain and could not sleep.

We were however ready to leave at 600 am and got to the hospital on time. They checked us in and we were ready for her spinal tap but she was very agitated and would not keep still, so the spinal tap was postponed. We then went to the fourth-floor to begin her first week of intensified immunotherapy. She was given three new medications to be taken while she was getting this therapy. The whole process took four-hours, we sat and watched our daughter receive her first infusion. Once we finished, she was really tired and just wanted to sleep. We got back to Moss and I updated them on the day. Janai slept well that night but had difficulties waking up for her therapy sessions the next morning.

We now had to figure out the best schedule for her after her appointments at CHOP. I had to get myself together and manage the new medication times, her therapy sessions, and the recent issue we had with her transport. I felt under attack in every direction, and I knew that I could not fail or fall. I prayed for strength to continue this journey. I found myself getting quiet and just listening for direction from God. When I opened my eyes I felt at peace and I began saying, "Thank you, Thank you, Thank you." I did this the rest of that day as I handled issue after issue. The nurse brought in the wrong medication. I had asked that every time they walked in to please announce themselves and what they were administering to my daughter. The nurse did that and was giving Janai the wrong dosage. I asked her to go back and check the notes and come back again. This time she did and had the correct dosage and apologized. I shared with her that they added something new and that she must check a patient's chart for new medication updates. This was something else I had on my list to discuss with the medical team. I always felt that I had to speak up about everything, and that day was just the beginning.

I had made several calls that morning to the Vice President of Moss Rehab, the Facilities Director, and the Nurse Manager. There was going to be a meeting in room 488, and I was angry! We had arrived in the lobby of Moss that morning to be transported in a raggedy van with no working seat belts. I had to tie my daughter in her seat using two broken straps and hold her while we were driving to CHOP. I was so upset but knew I had to get there on time and safely. I prayed the entire ride, and everyone in the van knew how upset I was. The week before, the van had two large holes in the floor that I had to cover with my foot to keep the rain from coming in. I had summoned everyone to this meeting and I said one word, "lawsuit." They all looked at me and said nothing. I then said think about this, "Moss Rehab puts a child under their care in an unsafe van with no working seat belts going to CHOP for immunotherapy treatments." Imagine the front page of every local newspaper and news outlet with that headline. Can you see it with me? I was outraged and said, "I am here taking care of my daughter and now I have to do all of your jobs! Give me the name of your fleet company, because I am calling them too!" I put everyone on blast that day, I was so done with the administrators at Moss, and they didn't know what to do with me. I also suggested that they create a Moss Rehab checklist for every transport that leaves this facility to ensure that the vehicles are safe for all patients. We might have been the first who needed this kind of medical accommodations, and hopefully we made them better for the next patients who might need them.

After our meeting, I was sent letters of apology and guaranteed that this would not happen ever again. I spoke with the president of the fleet company and gave them the same lecture and said that those vehicles are not fit for anyone, and should not be in service. To everyone's surprise our next car service to CHOP was in a black SUV with all the bells and whistles, and a new driver who referred to me as "The Boss Lady." Once this got around, several caregivers and staff would tell me the complaints on the floor because rumor had it, I could get it done. What a week it had been and it was only Wednesday.

I continued with my meetings with Janai's rehab team to get bi-weekly updates on her progress. She was progressing, but still was not where we all needed and wanted her to be. My baby still had a long way to go and I knew she would get there eventually. We had just started the treatments again, and I knew it would take some time, and time is what I had. I spent the weekend at home with Jayla and she was getting stronger with each visit and I could see a difference in her.

That following week started off great. Janai was eating better and doing more things that offered me glimpses of my daughter and brought me hope. Our weekly visits to CHOP were good as Janai received her second treatment. All of her lab work and ultrasound came back with good results. She was tolerating the chemo well and everything seemed to be working out in our favor. It seemed that way just for a day. I had another meeting with Nicole, one of the nurse managers because of the care we were receiving and the gossip I was hearing on the floor about my child and other patients.

My concerns:

1. Janai's care as a patient and how they viewed her
2. Communications between therapist and staff
3. Rehab and medical conditions, the differences between the two
4. Everyone on the same page about the care of Janai
5. More physical activities for Janai
6. Clarity about policies and procedures

I went over each one of these with her and she agreed that my concerns were legitimate. She agreed that I was a big help in the care of my daughter. It was difficult to be part of this team approach when we were dealing with rehab and medical together. However, I told her and the staff we would work together, as a team to achieve the best outcome for Janai. That week she began her physical therapy riding a bike and doing more strenuous exercises, which she enjoyed. She did a powerpoint with her occupational therapist, and staff was very proud of her progress. I encouraged them to push her because she was ready. I believed that the second round of immunotherapy treatments were beginning to put the flames out in her brain, and Janai was slowly coming back to us.

That next week started off well, but I noticed her appetite was out of control. To determine what was triggering this problem, I started looking at all of her medications; when she started them, the dosage and the times they were administered. She was always hungry and became very aggressive. I was very concerned about this new behavior. I immediately had her diet changed to more fruit and vegetables with no sugars. I asked for her thyroid to be checked and her glucose levels as well. I knew the staff was sick of my demands, but I continued taking care of my daughter and doing my best as her mother.

That Tuesday we got ready to go to CHOP for our third immunotherapy treatment. The car service was working out well and our new driver was kind and accommodated our every need. He arrived on time and always greeted us with a smile. He informed me that he was one of the managers and was asked personally to be our transport driver while we were at Moss. We were all concerned about Janai going to CHOP that day because she was just not herself, but she did well and we both made it through.

That week might have been one of her worst weeks at Moss. It took a lot out of everyone to control her behavior and her obsession with food. Janai would look at the clock and when it said 7 am, 12 noon and 6 pm she was ready for her meals and when the meals were over she was ready for snacks. This behavior went on all day and night. The staff could not have snacks in their pockets because she would grab them. I had to do something as I figured out what was causing this abnormal behavior. I decided to remove the clock from the room while she was at therapy and the nurses said,

"Wow, we would not have thought of that." I just laughed and kept on doing what I was doing, being a mother. After several days of watching and recording my daughter's behavior, the medical team and I agreed that it was a reaction to one of the medications. We did not stop it completely, but lowered the dose to .5mg. I prayed that this was the cause of my daughter's behavior change.

This medical journey back to joy was taking me in places that only God could get me through. I cried a lot that week and one day in particular, I could not stop the tears from falling. It was Good Friday, March 29, and I was overcome with such emotions. God gave his one and only son so we could have eternal life. I thought about what God did to save all of us in this world, and I began grieving. It was another feeling that I could not explain, but I knew it was God and I had to trust and continue to believe in the plan for my family.

That weekend I spent time alone at home while Jayla was visiting Angel in Florida for her spring break. I knew my daughter needed to get away from all of us, and have some fun in the sun. I returned back to Moss early that Monday and everyone was happy to see me. It seemed that Janai acted totally different with her father on the weekends. She knew who to act out with and her mother was not the one. I quickly got back to work preparing for our fourth trip to Chop. The medical team and I also decided to stop the medication that I had suspected was causing Janai's increased appetite and behavior changes.

Janai finished her fourth round of immunotherapy and continued tolerating everything well. Janai liked our visits to CHOP, and they all looked forward to seeing her. We made lots of new friends there, and I prayed for them all. It was quite humbling sitting there watching all of these beautiful souls fighting all kinds of illnesses. Many of them were diagnosed with cancer, sickle cell, thalassemia and bone marrow disorders. I tried to hold back tears when walking through this room as I looked at all the families fighting for their children. I thanked God for all of the medical teams and "White Coats," eventhough I had issues with some of them. It takes all of us to help in the healing of others.

Later that week I had another meeting with the nurse managers regarding Janai's care. Many of the nurses and CNA's(certified nursing assistants) were still not understanding Janai's illness and were therefore unaware of how to treat her. It was exhausting, but I was determined to make them all understand. Many of the patients on the floor were not as active as Janai and because she did not suffer a trauma to the brain from an accident; they were all confused about "why" she was there. The nurses were a little more knowledgeable but the "one to ones" and the CNAs were not. So they were all going to learn today about anti-NMDA receptor encephalitis. There were several whom we became close to, and I always explained Janai's illness with them and they all called her a miracle. I started seeing Janai become more independent and her appetite decreased. I knew that had something to do with the medication being stopped, but also I believed that my daughter was showing signs of healing.

The Awakening

There is a mighty power in your prayer.

April 4, marked the beginning of an awakening for Janai. She had slept well, woke up on her own, took her shower, got dressed, and ate breakfast. After receiving her daily medication and speech and physical therapies, one of our "one to ones" braided Janai's hair and she was happy. The look on everyone's face was priceless, as they had never seen Janai so active and engaged. That evening Damita came to visit along with Carvon and Jayla. It was a very special night, and I knew something spiritual was about to happen. It was just a feeling that I had all that day. Damita asked all of us to gather around Janai's bed to pray. I purposely left the door open as we prayed for the healing of my daughter's body, and every soul on that floor. Many walked by and stood at the door to watch us praying as a family over Janai as she laid still and very calm in the bed.

There was power in that room that night, and I will never forget how I felt as we prayed. Even now, I get chills thinking about it. Janai never spoke that evening and after everyone left she fell asleep in my arms. I held my daughter all night as I had done plenty of times during this medial journey. As tears rolled gently down my face, I continued praying for complete healing of her body. When Janai awoke on Friday, April 5, seventy-two days exactly, I was sitting in the chair dressed for the day and to my surprise, I heard these beautiful words come out of her mouth; "Good morning Mommy, when are we going home?" She said it with such clarity, excitement, and Joy that I stared at her in silence for a moment, not believing what I had just heard. She said it again as she got out of bed to go get her shower without any help from anyone. The nurses were so happy to see and hear Janai, the beautiful girl, I had always spoken about.

That was an awakening day to remember, and after all of her therapies were finished, we took a long walk outside. The grounds were so beautiful, the sun was shining and the trees were all in bloom. We walked up the hills and all around the property. She was laughing and talking the entire time. I just kept thanking God for the healing process and for that day, one day at a time. I stayed with Janai that weekend as she continued improving and we continued our long walks outside, as walking became something she enjoyed, and looked forward to. The fresh air was medicine to both of us. I began to breathe again and this time my tears were tears of Joy.

Janai had several visitors that weekend; Uncle Ross, Uncle James, Aunt Tina, Aunt Shelly, cousins Jordyn and Ryan. They brought her lunch, cards, and her favorite Rita's water ice. She was so happy to see them all. She cried when they all left and asked again "Mommy, when are we going home?" I said with confidence "soon my love" and she smiled with that beautiful smile I had so missed. I knew if she continued healing this way, she would be going home soon.

What would that look like was the question I often asked myself. It was already April and she had missed almost the entire half of the school year. She missed the Jack and Jill Teen Conference, her class trip to Orlando and other important events during her senior year. I knew she would ask me about them all at some point, once she regained her memory. I was thinking too much into everything and had to get myself together and remember "one day at a time." I had trusted God and continued trusting the process, no matter what the outcome looked like. My faith was much stronger than my current circumstances.

Monday morning came and our beautiful Janai continued progressing well. We had now incorporated outdoor walks as part of her regular therapy, and Janai looked forward to going outside. Again, I could begin to see the sparkle come back in my daughter's eyes. This particular day she asked me, "Why did this happen to me?" and looked right at me waiting for an answer. I told her that sometimes things happen that we have no control over and how we must always trust God for the outcome, no matter what that might be. I also told her that there is a blessing coming from this. I don't think she grasped what I was saying, but I knew one day she would understand what a blessing she would become to many who would meet her. Psalm 77:14 "You are the God who performs miracles, you display your power among the people." I have always believed that Janai was a miracle since birth, and I still believe that to this day.

On April 9, we did not have our regular scheduled appointment at CHOP, so Janai went to all of her therapies and actually finished her homework, which was to remember all of her teachers and the classes they taught in her senior year. Debbie, her speech therapist, was so excited to see the improvement from Janai and was more excited in seeing her smile and her laugh. Janai had made so many improvements that she was now cooking and doing laundry without any problem during her OT therapy. I was so proud of her and I could see that she was working hard to get her life and joy back. The weather had been so nice that I took every opportunity to take Janai outside and I believed that she knew she was getting ready to go home soon.

It had been very hot that month in April and many of the patients had complained about how uncomfortable they all felt in their rooms, especially at night. I was walking back from the cafeteria and saw all the rooms with fans in them. Even Janai and I complained about how hot it was. By now, I hope you would have guessed that everyone had complained to me to make something happen very quickly.

I called the Assistant Vice President of Moss to complain about the air quality and the health benefits of the patients, staff and visitors. They knew who I was immediately and needless to say, the air conditioner was turned on several weeks earlier than scheduled. It was a heatwave during April 2013. Robyn the caretaker and the caregiver had her Super M.O.M Cape on one last time at Moss Rehab. Everyone was happy that the air was on and the patients were more comfortable. I had seen and heard many things that broke my heart, and if I could do anything that could make just a small difference, I was going to do it. My time spent at Moss was one that I would never forget, and the many families I bonded with, I will cherish forever.

The rest of that week went well, however, I noticed a glazed look on Janai's face and her therapist saw it too. We all agreed that Janai was trying so hard to do everything that was asked of her that she was getting physically and mentally tired. I suggested that she rest between her therapies, and I would watch her behavior.

I went home that weekend because I was mentally, physically and spiritually exhausted. I also knew that I had an appointment with Janai's counselor at Council

Rock High School that Monday morning. I saw my sister Tina and brother-in-love James on Saturday and was so grateful to them for always checking in to make sure I had what I needed over my weekend trips home. On Sunday, my sister-girlfriends, Carla, Roz, Karen, and Kathleen brought over dinner for the two of us. They all blessed me with words of encouragement, prayers and support. In retrospect, it was God that had orchestrated that much needed weekend of love from them all.

Monday morning I got up early and fixed breakfast for Jayla and took her to school. I always loved my special time with my baby girl, and I knew it was becoming difficult for her to say goodbye. I assured her that Janai was getting much better and would be coming home soon and we would all be a family again. My meeting with Mr. R went well as I was well aware of homebound instructions, which Jayla had during the 2009-2010 school year. My ask to him was that Janai would walk with her class of 2013, and we would set up homebound instructors in Math, Science, and English. Janai had already fulfilled all of her requirements to graduate. This mother had a plan for her child, and I would use all my resources to make it happen. The school wanted to hand Janai her diploma and be done with her and me, and to their surprise I said "NO." Janai would get private lessons at home the rest of the school year and summer. This is how we were going to complete my daughter's senior year, she was still a student in the district. When you have been in the hospital for over 80 days, you have a lot to think about and a lot of work to get done. I did my homework and was ready for anything and everything they threw at me. I left the meeting getting exactly what Janai deserved as I continued to prepare for her arrival home.

April 16, was our rescheduled day at CHOP for our fifth treatment. We met with both Dr. Ryan and Dr. Sievert, who were very pleased with Janai's progress and felt that she was ready to be discharged from Moss and to continue her healing at home. This was an answered prayer. We discussed outpatient rehab as well as homebound instruction during the summer, all were part of the healing plan. They wanted to see her in four to five weeks for another treatment and a CT Scan.

That night Janai and I talked about next steps as I was very confident that she would be discharged from Moss and heading home to begin her new journey. I could tell she was anxious and I assured her "one day at a time." She didn't know how her friends would accept her and how she would begin to get her life back. My heart ached as she shared her concerns and fears with me. She had missed so much and had gone through even more. I told my daughter that God was with her and would continue to see her through this journey. I reminded her of how strong she was becoming and to always remember that she had a mighty village of people praying for her.

On April 18, we spoke to the medical team about Janai's discharge from Moss. I then started making calls setting up for homebound instructions and coordinating her outpatient rehab therapies. I wanted her to stay with Moss as they were familiar with her needs. Of course, I had to fight with our insurance company for continuity of service. They approved one of the two rehabs that she needed. I stayed on the phone going back and forth until they approved what I had requested. Janai would receive speech and occupational therapy as an outpatient at Moss Rehab. I called that victory for Team Johnson!

Another call I had to make was to our District's IU; a program called "Brain STEPS." A nationally recognized brain injury school and consulting program developed in Pennsylvania for students up to age nineteen. I wanted all the brain injury support and resources available for my daughter. I was connected with Sara, who became a great resource for Janai. I wanted Janai to start homebound immediately, but I needed the instructors to know a little more about her illness beforehand and what my expectations were. I also had to speak with Barbara the outpatient scheduler at Moss to get Janai's rehab scheduled. Janai was scheduled on Tuesdays and Thursdays from 2-4 pm for her rehab. This was progress and I felt good with the plan.

Everyone was excited that Janai was finally coming home after being in the hospital for eighty-five days. That day was long but much was accomplished and all I could think about was getting by baby home. Carvon, Jayla, and many friends got the house all ready for her return and brought all of her favorite food, flowers, and many gifts. I did ask that we have our privacy for the first couple of days and no company as she needed to get adjusted to being back home.

On April 18, I was up at 5:30 am dressed and ready as we all had prayed for this day to come. I had many emotions leading up to that day and now it was finally here. Janai got up around 6:45 am and just looked at me with tears in her eyes and asked "if she was dreaming," I said, "no sweetheart, you are not dreaming." She then asked, "Mommy, am I really going home today?" and I smiled and said "Yes Janai, we are going home." I saw in my beautiful daughter that morning all of her strength, determination, hope, and most important her JOY! The staff was in and out of our room saying their goodbyes and well wishes. I was too busy taking down the many get well cards, pictures, notes and other memorable items from the Team Johnson wall of healing and love. This wall reminded Janai who she was, and how many people were praying for her and loved her. Every day I would read a card or talk about something on that wall. The staff would love to hear about our strong village and commented on how loved and supported we were as a family. I carefully put everything neatly in a box knowing that one day Janai might want to read them in her voice and feel the love and support all over again.

I then gathered all of her clothes as well as mine from the tiny closet that was ours for fifty-eight days. I looked at those same three sweat suits that I wore every day and knew once I got home, I would never wear them again. I had to chuckle when looking at the brown one, even at Moss they knew if I had that one on with my leopard slippers, I was having a meeting in my room. Everything was packed, so I decided to go and say my goodbyes to the parents and caretakers of the many patients, with whom I had become very friendly with. I made sure they all had my personal phone number to call me at any time for love and support. I told them that I would stop by and see them when I brought Janai for her outpatient rehab. My heart was heavy as I looked at all of the patients on the fourth-floor, all of whom I had prayed for. The paperwork was done, the room was all packed up, we said our goodbyes, and as a family we walked out of Moss Rehab with our beautiful daughter on her Miracle Journey Back to Joy.

The Comfort of Home

There's no place like home,
it's where beautiful memories begin.

Janai was finally home and so happy to be in familiar surroundings. She was very quiet for the first couple of days and did not want to see anyone right away; however, she did want to get her hair done. I was very happy with that decision and made that appointment right away with our hair stylist Monique, who had been a true blessing to our family throughout this journey. She had been doing Janai's hair since she was five-years old and Janai's illness had been very difficult for her as well. She opened her salon early that day and did Janai's hair in privacy. That weekend we stayed in and watched all of Janai's favorite movies, and I continued to monitor my daughter's behavior. I knew the sooner I got her back into her normal routine, the better she would be.

We had our first outpatient rehab on April 23, from 9-11 am and it went well. The following days were busy with other appointments and visiting places she loved. I was determined to keep her active and not let her fall into a state of depression. This family had been through so much and if I was the one to keep the joy in the house, that was what I was going to do and Joyful Living became my new Mantra.

137

The first couple of weeks home Janai and I were busy coordinating her weekly schedule, She would have homebound instructions on Monday, Wednesday, and Fridays and rehab on Tuesday and Thursdays. My head was spinning because I also had to coordinate Jayla's eye appointments and Carvon's doctor appointments. My husband was still home on disability and was having good and bad days. Depression can take a major toll on a family and a marriage, especially if there are many other crises going on at the same time. Carvon was trying very hard to be happy for Janai, but he was still battling himself. I continued to keep the faith and pray for my husband and our marriage.

My calendar was very colorful and busy, but I made sure I had time for myself. A common question that was always asked, "Who takes care of you?" My main source of strength was my relationship with God. No matter what was going on, I stayed prayed up and obedient to God's word. I was human and made sure that I did my self care and kept my hair and nail appointments, a massage when I could, and my special chocolates in the freezer. On Fridays, I would always buy fresh flowers to brighten up my kitchen and bedroom, it's the small things that brought me joy.

May would be a big month for Janai, her eighteenth birthday and her senior prom was all approaching. Even though she never expected her senior year to look like this, I was determined to make it all happen for her. As we traveled back and forth to Moss, I used to see a dress shop called "Yes to the Dress" located in Huntingdon Valley, PA. Janai's senior prom was on her mind, and I could see the disappointment in her face, she thought about having to miss out on another important event. The prom was Saturday, June 1, and we only had three weeks before that date. After one of our sessions at

Moss, we stopped in that dress shop and I asked for the owner, but she was not there that day. I made an appointment for May 14, at 4:45 pm. On that Tuesday after our Moss visit, Janai and I walked into this beautiful boutique and met the owner Madison, whom I knew immediately, I would love. After Janai informed her that we were looking for a prom dress for June 1, she looked at us and said, "impossible to get a dress ordered and altered in less than two weeks." However, after I shared Janai's story, Madison, who began to cry, asked Janai to pick out the dress she loved and she would do everything in her power to make it happen. She became part of "Team Johnson" and we named her our "Prom Angel." That afternoon we all cried and hugged one another and were reminded again that nothing is impossible when you believe and trust God.

Madison ordered that dress, and on May 16, she called to inform us that the company had the dress, which was delivered and altered to fit Janai perfectly in time for her senior prom. When I went to pay for the gown, she said to me, "You are surrounded by "Prom Angels" it's already paid for. To this day we do not know who blessed us, but I want to say "thank you" to all the "Angels" who made Janai's dream come true that day.

On May 24, Janai's 18 birthday, started off with breakfast, a massage, hair and nails, and then a family dinner to celebrate our beautiful miracle daughter. I could see the joy coming back to her slowly. She was gaining her confidence back the more she believed in herself. I was patient with her and had to tell others to do the same as she was still healing.

On June 1, Janai was able to attend her senior prom thanks to so many family and friends who loved her. I had a big celebration at the house and invited everyone to her big send off. Uncle James chauffeured them to the party bus as we all followed. She looked amazing in her blue prom gown and was so happy to be around her friends who welcomed her back with love and support.

Janai had gone back to Council Rock to see some of her teachers and friends as many were getting ready for graduation. Janai was able to attend her senior BBQ, senior awards night, the graduation luncheon, and all the rehearsals leading up to that big day. June 19, 2013 my beautiful daughter walked across the stage to accept her high school diploma. There was a "Janai Johnson" section on the field with all her family and friends that screamed her name when it was called. They had to stop calling the other names because you could not hear anything but applause for our miracle daughter Janai.

Janai's Godmother Angel and daughters Alana and Alexia flew in to surprise her and me. Our friend Arnita had a dream about Janai while she was hospitalized, and shared with me that God showed her Janai walking across three stages; this was the first one, June 19, 2013. The graduation party followed that Saturday, and I invited the entire village of school friends, Bucks County Jack and Jill, Dance Arts of Yardley, Christian Stronghold, CHOP, Moss, family and neighbors near and far. I wanted to thank everyone for praying, loving and supporting us through this medical journey. We could not have made it through if not for all of them. The look on Janai's face when she saw everyone there to celebrate her was such a blessing, and she thanked everyone as well with a hug and kiss.

Our appointments continued at CHOP for more treatments and follow ups, and each time they saw Janai they were in awe at her progress. I shared with them that she went to her prom and participated in her high school graduation. Her appointments at Moss continued all summer, and she would drive us there. I could not let her be afraid of living her life, so I gave her reasons and purpose to live every day. Her studies were going well with the home instructors with the hope that she would attend Bucks County Community College in the fall.

I was turning 50 that summer, and my dream family vacation to Hawaii was put on hold. Instead, I spent a girls only trip in Martha's Vineyard with my daughters, my dear sister friends, Damita, Roz, Carla, neice Sydney and our gracious host Aliya. Carvon did not join us for this trip and stayed home surrounded by many who loved him and was helping him through the many challenges he was overcoming. I needed to get away and would have loved to go by myself, but the girls needed this as well. We had a beautiful week walking on the beaches, eating lobster rolls, laughing, loving and living life. The Vineyard has always been our happy place and we were blessed.

When we returned from vacation, Janai pressed on to finish her homebound lessons, and I could see her strength and confidence coming back. In the fall we enrolled her in Bucks County Community College. Jayla was entering her last year at Newtown Middle school and was becoming a very independent child and looking forward to high school next year. We were very hopeful that her eye had settled with the oil bubble, and we would be able to reduce the amount of eye drops and visits with Dr. Park.

I still remained a very busy mom chauffeuring everyone to their appointments and activities. Both girls did well in school that year. Janai finished her first semester at Bucks County Community College with a 3.5 and we all could see how determined she was to continue this part of her journey. Carvon was still home on disability and he too was determined to win this battle of his journey. Our family looked okay, but we were still broken in many ways.

I was happy to see the New Year of 2014. Janai finished her second semester with a 3.8 and that fall she transferred to her dream college, Drexel University. Carvon and I were so proud of our daughter because we knew all that she had gone through to get there. She was truly a miracle for all to see. Carvon was beside himself because his daughter was attending his alma mater. Janai would commute every day to classes, and as her mother I needed to see how she handled the stress of being a full time student.

I eventually transferred all of her medical records to the University of Pennsylvania Hospital and was given the names of two "White Coates," Dr. Wynne, Primary Care and Dr. Lancaster, Neurology, both of them were very familiar with Janai's autoimmune disease. We were blessed to have them both on "Team Johnson." They were in awe with Janai's progress and her most recent acceptance into Drexel University. Things were going well for Janai, and it seemed that she was adjusting to her new normal the best way she knew how, one day at a time.

Jayla was still very active in bringing eye care and safety awareness to our school district. She had the opportunity to present her story to all of the Bucks County school nurses along with Dr. Kammi Gunton, whose specialty is Pediatric Ophthalmology. We were very honored that Dr. Gunton accepted our invitation to speak, and Dr. Park familiarized her with Jayla's injury. Mrs. Dana Daniels introduced Jayla to the group of 40 professionals, and it brought tears to my eyes because Dana was Jayla's elementary school nurse from Sol Feinstone. Dana and I had been working together to bring someone from Wills Eye to speak to the Bucks

County Association of School Nurses on this subject. Dr. Gunton exceeded everyone's expectations, she was that good. The feedback from the nurses was very positive and the information presented could possibly help prevent undetected eye traumas in school aged children and beyond.

Jayla navigated her first year of high school the same way she had done in middle school, bold and brave. We had everything in place for her 504 accommodations and the nurses were all aware of who she was before she even walked through the doors. We were now seeing Dr. Park monthly unless there was a need to see him more frequently. Her eye pressure was monitored and all of her teachers and other staff members knew the signs to look for; swelling of the eye, redness, and complaining of headaches. Jayla had a hall pass to the nurse's office for the entire time while she was in high school, and she used it to her advantage.

Dr. Park still did not want her to participate in gym or any contact sports, so she was exempt all four years of high school and was very happy. I started noticing that her eye began to droop, and I became concerned. Dr. Park had told me that his goal was to keep Jayla's eye viable for as long as possible. He was concerned as she got older that the eye might start to deteriorate because of all of the surgeries and complications. We never really spoke about what that would look like for her, but I had my thoughts.

In 2015 Janai finished her first year at Drexel and continued to excel. She hadn't had any seizures since CHOP nor had they found any teratomas in her ovaries. We were grateful for this great news, but little did we know another storm was coming.

Jayla was beginning to get really bad headaches, and the eye was getting infected more frequently. On

December 11, 2015, Jayla was in class and noticed that her eye was very sticky. She immediately left to go to the nurse's office. The nurse examined her and saw that a sticky discharge was coming from her eye. She became alarmed and called me right away. After I picked up Jayla from school, we went straight to Wills Eye ER. Jayla's cornea was leaking fluid, which was not good. We were sent to see Dr. Ayers, a Cornea Specialist who examined Jayla and his assessment was a perforated corneal ulcer of her right eye. Her eye was then bandaged once again and a lubricant gel had to be administered four times a day along with an ointment morning and night. I was used to giving her eye drops, so I was comfortable with doing this.

I brought Jayla home and kept her out of school until her eye was healed. We were also given the name of another doctor that we contacted for a consultation. I could tell that Jayla was thinking about, what we all never spoke about, until now. We followed up with Dr. Park in January of 2016, and as Carvon, Jayla, and I sat there, we listened to Dr. Park speak about Jayla's options. It was recommended that Jayla receive a cornea transplant; however, her lens were destroyed from the accident and if she received this transplant, there would be no guarantee that this condition would not occur again.

Her eye had been through so many traumas, and we were now faced with the only other option. Dr. Park and I had discussed this before and I had been praying for a miracle for Jayla, and I knew she was praying for one also. As we discussed Jayla's options, I could see her getting very upset and she began to cry. The nurse in the room also began to cry, and I put my arms around Jayla and whispered, "I love you and you will be ok, I promise." I had told Jayla this so many times, but this time I knew she would be ok. My daughter had been through so much, and now she was facing what she never wanted to hear, "The removal of her eye."

Dr. Park gave us the name of Dr. Penne, Chief of Oculoplastic and Orbital Surgery Service at Wills Eye Hospital. When we left that examination room, the whole office was quiet and the staff all hugged Jayla and me. I could see the tears in their eyes as we both walked past each one of them. This place had been our home for eight years, and they had remembered the little girl who lit up the office every Tuesday and made everyone fall in love with her. They wanted to believe a miracle would happen for her too. We came home that day with a lot to think about, and my heart was so heavy for my daughter. Jayla should have been thinking about prom, college visits and other exciting things while in high school, instead she was thinking about another major surgery that would change her life forever.

That evening Jayla cried and said "Mommy why did this happen to me?" I had heard her ask this to me too many times over the years. My answer was always the same; "God has a plan for you sweetheart, you are so strong, God will get you through this." If I believed this, then I had to believe for both of us, and I did just that. I saw how God was blessing this family in ways that no one would ever believe. Dr. Park told us that we did not have to make a decision right away and suggested that we at least make an appointment to meet Dr. Penne. Jayla had many questions, and I knew that I could not answer any of them, so she began to write them out. I told her that Dr. Penne would answer them all, which he did at our first appointment on February 16, 2016. Dr. Penne was fascinated with Jayla and showed great compassion as he listened to her concerns. She was very confused about an "enucleation," What does that mean?

He explained that it is the "removal of the eye", a procedure that leaves the eye muscles and remaining orbital contents intact. This type of ocular surgery is used for a number of ocular tumors in eyes that have suffered severe trauma and in eyes that are otherwise blind and painful. This information was a lot for Jayla to take in, but she listened and had several other questions to ask. I needed Jayla to feel comfortable, this was a life altering decision that would affect our daughter for the rest of her life. That year, we made several more appointments with Dr. Penne as Jayla had to get mentally prepared with the idea that she would be having another major surgery and that it could possibly be her last.

The other big question was "Once removed, what is put in its place?" Dr. Penne then gave us the name of an "Ocularist" a carefully-trained technician skilled in the arts of fitting, shaping, and painting ocular prostheses for people who have lost an eye or eyes due to trauma or illness. Once again, a lot to process, but we talked and prayed as a family before we made any decisions. I also knew if we were going to have this procedure, I would need to have all the information regarding insurance coverage for this kind of medical procedure.

Dr. Park called me one evening and we spoke about the benefits of this surgery for Jayla and I said, "I want to get this done before she goes away to college." I knew she would be able to handle the operation, but I also knew she would want a "prosthetic eye." The benefits for Jayla would be; no more eye drops, no monthly visits with Dr. Park, no concerns about eye pressure or other eye traumas. It would be a "new normal" for her. We gave her all the time she needed to wrap her brain around this decision and did not rush her. However, her eye pressure was beginning to get low again and the headaches started to cause her great pain. It always broke my heart to see her in such pain, but she still pushed through. Jayla never complained or wanted sympathy from anyone. She really was a strong young woman. I knew we would have to make a decision sooner rather than later. Dr. Penne had given me the names of two Ocularists in the area and also told me that they did not accept insurance. If I was to allow my daughter to get this surgery, you best believe she was also getting a prosthetic eye. I could not let her go through this operation and not feel good about herself. I had no idea how much it would cost, and I didn't care, my only concern was Jayla.

One morning I looked at both cards and began praying over which one to call. I knew nothing about either of them, only that Dr. Penne had recommended them and said they were the best. I picked up the phone one morning and called K. Kelly's office first. A very nice woman answered the phone and I began to tell her why I was calling. When she asked me what made you call us, I simply said "God." She chuckled and said, "God is on your side today because we don't accept insurance; however, I am going to accept yours and put it through as a medical claim." I began to cry as I said, "Thank you" and "God Bless you" over and over again with gratitude.

We made an appointment for Mr. K. Kelly and Jayla to meet. I wanted him to see Jayla and get to know her. He would give Jayla a little piece of what she thought was gone forever. The two met and like everyone else, he fell in love with her at first sight. He told her that he had never met anyone quite like her, and she replied, "I am one of a kind."

We were now ready to schedule the surgery and begin a new journey for Jayla. I wanted to wait until school was out so she could have the entire summer to heal physically, mentally and emotionally. I could not even imagine what was going through her mind as we approached Wednesday, June 22, 2016.

The Sunday before the surgery she had written a poem, and on our way home from church, she said she wanted to read the poem under the Wills Eye Sign and for us to record her. Once we got into Center City and parked the car, Jayla went underneath the sign to recite her poem. However, there was too much noise outside and we could not hear a word she said. I then walked and knocked on the closed door of the Wills Eye building. The guard looked at me through the large glass door and said, "We are closed." I smiled and said, "Please open the door" and she did. We were all dressed in our Sunday best, I like to believe that's what helped her open the doors to the hospital to three complete strangers. Once inside, I told her Jayla's story and she said to me, "I knew today was going to be special." She asked Jayla where she wanted to read her poem, and she decide on the wall that read **"NEVER IMPOSSIBLE"** and then she began reciting:

The Hourglass

The hourglass is filled with sand as it gets flipped from side to side. Time is ticking away. What has one person just lost? Have they lost their thoughts? Their sight even perhaps? Have they lost their childhood? Each child dreams of conquering the world and achieving great things. No child ever imagines losing something so dear to their body and maybe even "so small and complex." Within just a blink of an eye the hourglass got flipped to say for the better or for the worse? Only time will tell. Maybe we should go inside the hourglass to see what lies beneath the grainy sand. We travel back to the year 2009 the night is winding down and all is quiet and calm to say the least until a snap breaks out which now has just left a little crack on the hourglass. Only some pieces of the sand spills out, so what else comes out? Perhaps doctor appointments, endless nights in the hospital, multiple surgeries but even so the sight of someone with only being able to see sight out of one eye? But don't YOU worry; YOU can still see the hourglass unlike others. You can still see what is happening to your right, YOU can still see. SNAP! Another crack has been seen on the glass but this time more is spilling out: more surgeries, a jewelry line collection, home school bound, interviews, and the everlasting childhood has now been taken which is now sitting in the sand as time ticks away. The life this person once had is being shaped and formed very differently than anything anyone could have imagined. Fast forward to 2016. 7 years have gone by. Has the sight returned? Has the glass still been spilling out sand and little clues? Will the glass ever be replaced? Each month of the 12 months brings a new challenge. It's June exactly June 22 and the hourglass has been magically fixed. Has the vision? Has surgery occurred? Has the damaged eye been replaced by a new eye to make sure there are not anymore snaps in the hourglass. Time is still ticking. 7 years from now where will the hourglass and the girl be? Achieving greatness, making memories that her childhood never got to see? Time waits for no one, so what does your hourglass show?

After Jayla read the last line, we all were in tears. She had not read this to anyone, so I was just as amazed as the security guard and Janai. This was so moving and healing for her. Our new friend was touched and told Jayla she couldn't wait to see what God was going to do with her life. I still have chills thinking of that afternoon and watching my baby read what she kept inside for all these years. Janai was able to record that poem and the night before her surgery, I had asked for prayers and posted the video on my Facebook page for all to see and hear. The response was overwhelming and she felt the love and support from everyone.

That morning at the hospital, we did as we always did before any of Jayla's surgeries. We prayed over her and for everyone who came in contact with her. Jayla had asked for Beyonce to be played in the operating room. They agreed and accommodated all of her wishes. The surgery went well and as Jayla was in the recovery room, I looked up and Joe Bilson the CEO of Wills, Dr. Park, and Dr. Haller all had come to visit Jayla. The nurses wondered why the CEO and the Chief of Staff were on the floor. "Who were they visiting?" Those that knew said "Our VIP Jayla Johnson." Everyone was so kind and loved caring for Jayla while she was there.

Jayla came home that evening, but earlier that week, our central air stop working and we were getting a new unit put in the next day. I could not have my baby resting uncomfortably in this heat, the diva does not like to be hot. So, we went to stay at the home of Rosalind and Don, our dear family friends, who treated her like a princess. It was so cute to see their dog Giovanni lay at her bedside and watch over her as she recovered. I can not thank our village enough for all the love and support they showed us during this journey with Jayla.

The rest of that summer Jayla continued healing before she would be fitted for her new prosthetic eye. She was given a temporary one first until the making of the new one. During this process she would have to sit for several hours with a break, while he worked on the fitting, shaping, and painting of the prostheses to match her eye perfectly. It was exciting to watch this process.

During that time Jayla had to learn to take the eye out and clean it. This took some practice for both of us. Her new prosthetic eye was ready in late August, just before she started her junior year in high school. We went to the office and he showed Jayla her eye and to my amazement, it looked perfect. I really could not tell that it was a prosthetic, it looked so real.

Jayla became self conscious at first when she went back to school, but no one said anything to her, that's because most of her friends just saw Jayla. She began to adjust well in taking care of her eye which she named, "Eyelean." Our follow up visits that summer with Dr. Penne went well, and he was very pleased with the final results. Jayla was still getting used to the eye and complained that it felt heavy. We scheduled another appointment with K. Kelly and he was able to correct "Eyelean" by smoothing the rough edges down and making it more comfortable for Jayla. After a year with her new prosthetic, she got an infection under her eyelid and Dr. Penne was able to fix it with no problems. Jayla had a few stitches but they dissolved and you could not see any scars, which made her very happy.

Her junior year began with a frightened young girl, facing the reality of losing her eye, but she would never lose her vision for life. The end of the year my daughter attended her junior prom with her good friend Eric. Jayla's makeup was done by a family friend Mia, and she took exceptional care especially around Jayla's eyes that you couldn't tell one was a prosthetic. This was the first time since the accident that Jayla didn't wear her glasses and she said, "Mommy, I just want to be me." At that moment I saw my daughter's strength, heard her voice and I knew she was going to be fierce and unstoppable.

2018-Joyful Living

Joy will take you places
happiness will never find.

For Jayla's senior year, she ran for class president, started a club called V.O.I.C.E. (Voices of Inequality at Council Rock Every Day), brought together a movement to bring more diversity and training to The Council Rock School District, interviewed with several local papers, appeared on TV, and spoke on the floor of Congress about the hate in her school and community. In 2018 Jayla graduated from Council Rock North High School with several awards and a bright future ahead of her.

Jayla B. Is currently a senior in the Pennoni Honors College at Drexel University, and is majoring in Entertainment and Arts Management with a minor in Business Administration. Jayla has grown through these trials and is looking forward to seeing what God will do next in her life.

In 2018 Janai B. graduated from Drexel University with a Bachelor of Science in Business Administration and a concentration in Marketing. We all watched her walk across that second stage. Janai is currently working as a Marketing Professional and living her best life. Only God knows what that third stage will be.

By 2018 Carvon had overcome his depression and speaks about his medical journey with his support groups. He is working full time, enjoying his family, playing lots of golf and is grateful to be alive.

The beautiful baby girl that the young couple named Robyn; which means "Bright Fame" is excited to share this God inspired book with each of you. Faith led me to walk this journey and trusting God gave me the strength to live it, and today I am Living Joyfully.

About the Author

Joyful Living

Robyn Scott-Johnson is a Wife, Mother, Sister, Activist, Advocate, Teacher, Caregiver, Lifestyle Coach, Community Leader, Encourager and has over 35 years of sales and marketing in the pharmaceutical, radio and hospitality industries. Her most rewarding job has been a Mother to her beautiful daughters Janai and Jayla.

Made in the USA
Middletown, DE
04 June 2023